Political Emancipation

Observations of a Black Man Who Rejected Liberal Indoctrination

Volume 1

D0901805

Political Emancipation

Observations of a Black Man Who
Rejected Liberal Indoctrination
Volume 1

BY

Andre Harper

Bookstand
Publishing
www.BookstandPublishing.com

Published by
Bookstand Publishing
Morgan Hill, CA 95037
2993_6

ISBN 978-1-58909-627-1

Printed in the United States of America

ACKNOWLEDGEMENTS

I dedicate this book to my mother. She was 16 when I was born. She didn't know or have much back then but she did the best she could to provide for me. I think she did a pretty good job. Mama, I love you always.

Kelley DeLane Lewis

June 16, 1960 - October 31, 2007

Also to my wife, my grandfather, children, and family for their patience and support; my longtime friends and new friends discovered during the writing and publishing of this work.

To the many Americans who still believe that our Constitution as well as our dear Republic is worth preserving and defending!

Table of Contents

1

THE PURPOSE OF THIS BOOK

The longer I work in the political realm and the more I expose my conservative values, I find that as a black man, liberals will only accept me if I entertain them or obey them. It doesn't matter to them if I make a fool of myself or am unable to effectively communicate an intelligent position on things other than who was going to win the championship. In fact, the more informed and articulate I present myself on positions they disagree with, the angrier and more vicious they treat me. It's as if they expect me to be a fool and get mad when they find out I refuse to depend on the direction from some appointed black leader while I embrace my independent thought and reasoning. Now you will find that when black people earn an education and are willing to challenge them intellectually, they have no other recourse than to attack our character and reputation while never bothering to understand our rationale or how we come to certain conclusions. The point is that in the liberal mind, black people have a specific place. That place is one of subservience and subdued thinking.

The purpose of this book is for the reader to explore the perspective and experience of a black man in the United States who is proud to be black and proud to be an American. This is the story of a patriot who will gladly defend his freedom and constitution for the rights it protects. I am not here to offer the meaning of life or provide answers to all of the problems that ail our society or the black community. However, through the process of elimination, I can tell you that the government is not the answer. Somewhere the answer lies in the individual and a collective desire to preserve our Republic. Perhaps if all Americans take advantage of the freedom the constitution affords as I did, we can recognize that despite philosophical differences, the desire to maintain our society should remain the focus because regardless our differing opinions on gay marriage, abortion or taxation. If we are invaded or enslaved by a hostile enemy, I can assure you that these things will not matter to them. Each person must realize there is a price for freedom. Each of us must learn our history, how it operates, the rights it affords us and that we must remain eternally diligent because there will always be those who will threaten it.

My Realization

I'll admit it. I was naïve. I was a young man who put faith and trust into contemporary Black leadership. Why wouldn't I? I never asked myself why the intellectual leaders in my community were always the clergy or so-called civil rights leaders. That's just the way it was. I believed that Jesse Jackson was the leader of Black people, our spokesman and representative to the world at-large. Why shouldn't he be? He ran for president. I trusted that these men of God and people who had emerged to lead had clean hearts and my best interest in mind. Boy was I wrong.

At some point in my life, I began to observe things, listen, collect information, and contrast what was being done to what was being said. Then I would look at the results of those actions. Amazingly, as I matured, I realized that there are many forces moving around us. I learned that although we like to consider ourselves civilized in the 21st century, we follow the same laws as the animals in the Serengeti or the Mohave Dessert and that only the strong and most prepared survive. It may not be the nicest thing, it may not be politically correct to say, but it's the truth. All human beings must be willing to make sacrifices in order to survive especially in the United States. No group of people should be exempt from hard work or the laws of nature. Liberals constantly try to repeal laws of nature which only seem to make their solutions much worse than the problem ever was. This should be a rule universally accepted. Unfortunately, through political calculations, African Americans and many others the liberals like to label as "disenfranchised" people have been led astray by the Democratic Party in order to subdue their ambition for political gain. Over the last two generations no other group has benefited more from the collective ignorance of black people than the Democratic Party!

Through my maturation, I began to realize that my people are living on a political plantation courtesy of people like Howard Dean and Al Sharpton. Many black people are operating unconsciously with the blind loyalty that only a slave can give to his master. While many can't confidently explain their loyalty or the positions their masters advocate, they will vehemently reject the opposition, even though they may agree with them more because they fear the proverbial chastening rod. The Democratic Party has created an environment in black community where the worst thing you can be is a Republican. When black people reject the Democratic Party and liberalism, they resort to using their chastening rods for reprimand. These chastening rods include character assassination, turning the community against you simply because you disagree, marginalizing your opinions, attacking your livelihood, and (as I found out first hand during my campaign) intimidation.

You Make Up Your Own Mind

The purpose of this book is not to persuade black people to become Republicans but to put the African-American vote in play, making it competitive for both parties. Although I consider myself a Republican, the goal of this book is for my community to become independent thinkers and independent voters. Then we should leave the Democratic Party's plantation and hold them accountable for the atrocities that they have committed against the black community for generations. Although I have found that changing the minds of black people is harder then squeezing orange juice from a tomato, I will present my case the best way that I can.

Before you delve into this book, I believe that it is important that you understand my background and perspectives. According to liberal talking points (and John Edwards)[1], I should be incarcerated or dead. I should not be publishing a book about the crimes that the Democratic Party has perpetrated against their most loyal constituency. Nonetheless, this book presents observations and conclusions based on my experiences that I believe are accurate. I am a firm believer that opinions are like noses, everyone has one. No one's nose is more important than another's. However, you must be interested in my opinion. I am grateful and humble that you are willing to learn more. My positions will be supported by facts and actual occurrences, not emotion conjuring rhetoric liberals depend on to control behavior. Unlike liberals, I don't focus on intent. I could care less. I am only concerned with results. You don't get any credit from me for good intentions when they result in destruction.

I am not claiming to be an expert on Constitutional Law but I have read the Constitution a few times and believe in what it says. I am appreciative of the rights afforded by this document with the full knowledge that when it was drafted it didn't include me. I must first pay homage to the Republican Party of the 1860's who felt it necessary to include all American men in the Constitution despite the fierce opposition from the Democratic Party. Many would argue that the First Amendment is the primary building block of the freedom that our nation enjoys. The First Amendment states "Congress shall make no law respecting an establishment of religion, or prohibiting the free exercise thereof; or abridging the freedom of speech, or of the press; or the right of the people peaceably to assemble, and to petition the Government for a redress of grievances."

When I decided to write this book it was important that I be blatantly honest. I will tell you exactly how I feel and describe my experiences that led me to various conclusions. I can't guarantee that you won't be offended, but I will guarantee that I will be honest. I would rather tell you the truth and have you be upset, than lie to you and have you lose respect for my integrity. As mentioned earlier, the First amendment guarantees me the right to print and say what I feel; despite this, you may not like what it is I say. Of course, this goes both ways. I respect liberals exercising their right to voice their opinions as well. My purpose is not to offend, but to be honest in the most tactful and respectful way possible with the knowledge that there will be people who disagree. However, if you do get offended, you will have to work that out on you own.

In my opinion, disagreement is a good thing because it allows people to see the same things differently. We are all born into different lives, so we all have different experiences which will often lead us to different conclusions. The challenge is accepting these differences, respecting these differences, and agreeing to disagree without being violently disagreeable as Dr. Martin Luther King so eloquently stated.

Many Black people have a romantic view of Africa. We like to think of Africa as a place where our brothers and sisters lived in harmony. A place where every man was a king and every woman was a queen. As the theory goes, then the evil European came to Africa, capturing everyone in sight and brought them to America to pick cotton. Of course this isn't entirely true. In truth, there was conflict in Africa long before a white face ever appeared on the scene. Tribes clashed and killed one another. They conquered and enslaved one another. Many of their enslaved were sold to Europeans for weapons and other valuable items. Once the European inserted his guns and way of life, things only got worse. Men have always resorted to violence. As long as there is limited land, limited resources and limited women, men will always find a reason to kill one another.

I learned that many people live their lives unconsciously. When I listen to the radio, watch television, read the newspaper, go to school, go to church, I began to notice that I was constantly bombarded with messages. Then I would mentally note conversations that I had with other people. Eventually, I noticed that behind every message there was purpose. The purpose could be genuine, out of concern, sinister or selfish but there was always a purpose. When my mother told me to clean up my room, it was to teach me the value of cleanliness. When my pastor told me about the blessing of serving God, it was in hopes of my soul being saved. When Hasbro told me about the new "Transformers line", it was in hopes that I would go out and buy them (and I did). Nonetheless, everyday we are constantly bombarded with messages. Unfortunately, the average person appears to be unwilling to navigate, decipher or challenge this constant barrage of communication. People react to this in many forms some of which can be very destructive. I have found through my experiences that not everyone is able to process all of these messages. In fact, many people seem unwilling to fight and just submit to them.

You Have Fun, We'll Do All of the Thinking

We live in a time where people are increasingly busy. Many people don't have the time or desire to do research, especially when it comes to politics. This does the voter and society a major disservice. People constantly complain about inaction, yet re-elect the same people. Politicians know this.

Many spend big money on consultants and pollsters who shape the messages and buzz words designed to trigger specific emotions and responses. As a former political candidate, I learned that people don't care about platforms. Politicians know that most people vote based on name identification, emotions, perception and message recall. Unfortunately for our country, the ranks of the uninformed and voters that depend others for direction appear to be increasing. This knowledge of an increasingly uniformed and ever dependent electorate allows politicians from the left to continue to increase their self-sustaining, big government agenda.

Americans don't have time to worry about dissecting the presidential candidate's platforms much less the platforms of the gubernatorial candidates, judges, county auditors or city council members. If you are for change, education, fairness and are against crime, then that's all people seem to care about. Americans would much rather spend their free thought space worrying about who entertainers are sleeping with, the hottest songs, who the next big celebrities are and planning how they are going to live once they become famous. All the while, Americans are being constantly bombarded with messages that tell us what to wear and when these garments are no longer acceptable. The messages tell us how to act. The messages tell us what to buy. The messages keep us focused on ourselves and not to worry or be concerned with what may be going on around us.

Others act as though they reject common misconceptions when in fact they become the poster child of it. For instance, the contemporary black man has embraced a violent, hedonistic and anti-social culture that has proliferated throughout the world. Many consider themselves thugs or goons. A thug is defined as a cruel or vicious ruffian, robber, murderer, and an aggressive and violent young criminal. I suppose if you look at the definition then thug is the appropriate description to accompany the behavior. Many our young men feel that they are defying the status quo by acting in this manner, and that they are unique. In fact, quite the opposite is true.

The Liberal Plan for Black Men

I have been fortunate to have been able to travel around the country and world. It doesn't matter if you are in Cincinnati, West Palm Beach, Atlanta, or Leesville, Louisiana. Drive through the black neighborhoods and you will see the exact same thing. You will find the corners filled with black men (young and old) dressed in white t-shirts engaged in unproductive activity. If you talk with many of them, I am sure they will tell you they are unique. If you talk longer you will find that their conversations are strikingly similar and that many are just clones, perpetuating the popular image of the contemporary black man made famous by music videos as life imitates art (and I do use art loosely.)

Too often I see young black men walking down the street wearing designer clothes and no belt only to constantly switch hands holding up their pants. If they could afford the clothes, surely they could afford the belt. That's not the issue. I believe that many don't pull their pants up because it is a sign of societal conformity. In a culture where being an outlaw is the norm, any sign of conforming could result in ridicule from peers. Ironically, the ones who do their best to exist outside of the mainstream culture operate in a manner where they cannot be distinguished.

If you are not familiar with the plight of African-Americans, you will simply accept this as black culture. Unfortunately, the biggest perpetrators of this abomination are black people who don't know their own history. I will address this later.

As a young black man, I realized early on that there was a stigma attached to me that was created by liberals in order to make the case for why then need to advocate on my behalf and get more program dollars to provide for me since socio-economics prevent me from doing these things for myself. These stereotypes include being athletic, hip, unruly, uncontrollable, inarticulate, ignorant, violent, hedonistic, lazy and arrogant. In order to advance their political agenda, liberals want you to believe the notion that we are born at a deficit in comparison to other ethnicities. We are even born at a deficit when you compare us to black women. We have become vilified. It doesn't take very long for a little black boy to learn this. In fact, once he starts to interact with others outside of his home, he realizes that he is different and society has a pre-established set of rules designed specifically for him. Understandably, many young black men buckle into the pressure early by accepting the role liberals have created for us. Many of us find it much easier to submit to the stereotype than to struggle and defy them. In my life I have met so many black boys with great potential who gave into the pressure and became statistics. Black male failure gives liberals a sense of comfort knowing that they have "disenfranchised" people to coddle while simultaneously increasing their voter rolls. Then there are the many other black boys born into privilege that aspire to become statistics because they don't want to be perceived as inauthentic. They fear the scorn many successful black receive from the community. This includes being called a sellout, an Uncle Tom or being accused of acting white.

To understand the tormented psyche of the black man, you have to go back to slavery and re-trace his steps to understand why the contemporary version behaves in such a manner. I will explore this later. This book is about my personal political odyssey and experiences leading to my departure from the Democratic Party. This has led to my political emancipation followed by my emergence as an independent thinker.

Through experience and scores of political conversations with other black people, I have concluded that black people have been conditioned to funnel all political conversations through party loyalty instead of ideals. It's like the Democrats have inserted an overseer inside of our heads that has to monitor our thoughts and approve what we say. The overseer won't allow any scrutiny of the Democratic Party to leave the mouth. Any disagreements will be immediately deleted from the cranium. They have also trained us to believe that EVERY other black person processes political thought this way. My political beliefs are guided by MY PERSONAL conservative beliefs and not the Republican Party. When the GOP is loyal to their party principles, I am a loyal supporter; when they abandon them, I will fiercely object and scrutinize them. As a result of my differing thought pattern, I have a difficult time having political conversations with other black people when I ask them to remove party and just discuss the merits of the issues. It seems as though the mind overseer won't allow them to engage. He must threaten them with the chastening rods I mentioned earlier.

These mind overseers have had a crippling effect on the dialogue in the black community. Issues tend to be more complex than just party line votes. Most importantly, it displays that Democrats not only control the votes of black people but the minds as well. These mind overseers won't allow blacks to even internally challenge Democrat policy or intentions in their own mind. The Democrat encroachment on the sanctity of thought is the epitome of mind control. Having confronted and ejected the mind overseer implanted by the Democratic Party allowed me to realize that I had been living on a political plantation and had not even realized it.

My Opposition to the Democratic Party

I'm not against people who claim to be Democrats, but I do oppose the institution of the Democratic Party and many of its tenets. On a personal level, I don't have a problem with people until they try to indoctrinate me with their beliefs or take issue with me exercising my constitutional rights. I have served this country and defended these rights for every citizen as an active duty soldier in the United States Army. Even had I not served in the military, I'm still afforded these rights because I am a natural born citizen. I also don't think that most liberals are bad people. In fact, I believe that they are people with good intentions that allow their guilt and perceptions of the world to limit their potential happiness. They are then easily manipulated by the power hungry liberal elite. They then force their beliefs on the rest of us. Many times their advances or attempts at charity are not needed or wanted. All too often their charity results in unintended consequences which result in permanent dysfunction that can take generations to correct. That's why I always say "beware of the do-gooders."

After looking at the Democrat mantra objectively and jettisoning the bias against Republicans that I inherited, I realized that the DNC's positions didn't make much sense to me. The pie in the sky rhetoric makes you feel good but it is notoriously impractical. When I think about some of the people that the Democratic Party sends into the Black community to promote their message, it further discredits their institution. What I have learned is that most of the institutions they promote are hypocritical, contradictory and racist.

Rep. Shelia Jackson Lee (D-TX) came to church at New Jerusalem in Cincinnati to campaign for Obama and the Democrats in 2008. She and her minions stopped to talk to me in the foyer probably assuming that my brown skin would make me receptive to their rhetoric. I was in the mood for some fun so I decided to play along and acted as if I didn't know who she was (even though I did.) After I acted unimpressed with her introduction, which I wasn't, she proceeded to tell me that John McCain and the GOP were racist and that their policies hurt African Americans. I asked her if when they pass laws, they made individual laws for each racial group and the laws for blacks harsher. She said no. She couldn't explain to me how the same laws apply to everyone else hurt us more. Then I pressed her to admit that she believed that blacks are therefore incapable of following the same rules as everyone else and of course she wouldn't. Regardless, race hustlers like her must assume they can walk up to any black person with that race baiting non-sense and expect us to follow them blindly. Unfortunately, it works and that's why they keep doing it.

I spoke on a panel for young black boys in order to introduce them to politics. It wasn't a debate but my friends at the Cincinnati 100 Black Men asked me to speak on behalf of Republicans and they asked another black male to speak on behalf of the Democrats. One of the young men asked us both what the differences are for both parties. I began by telling him that you could ask 10 different Republicans that question and they can give you 10 different answers, so I will answer based on my perspective. I told him that on a basic level Republicans believe in low taxes, limited government, strong national defense, and the strength of the individual. I also told them that personally, I want a government to pick up my trash, make sure bombs aren't being dropped on my head, and to leave me alone. My Democratic counterpart said that the Democrats will also make sure it that the trash is picked up, they will also make sure that bombs aren't being dropped on your head, and then he said that the key difference is that just in case you and your neighbor are unable to provide health care for your children then they will. He also said that Democrats believe that the rich should be taxed

16

higher than the poor. I could not have said it any better myself. I told the children not to get rich so they wouldn't get discriminated against by their Democrat friends because of their success.

In a campaign rally at the University of Dayton, the racist Democratic National Committee Chairman Howard Dean commanded that his minions go out and vote immediately. He told them that they haven't done their job if they don't also begin volunteering in their community. He then made a remark about taxes. "You can't trust Republicans with your money," Dean said. I agree.[2] I don't trust any bureaucrat with my money, especially him and his liberal cronies. Many conservatives understand this as well. That's why the GOP pushes for lowering taxes and allowing citizens to spend their own money and not let people like Dean waste it. However, you can trust that the Democrats will blow it or give it to someone that supports them. They will use your money to buy votes.

Legalized Discrimination

Democrats promote and encourage the redistribution of wealth. I believe that Democrats are worse than thieves when it comes to taxes. How can Democrats honestly advocate taking away earnings from people who make honest livings just because they feel you make too much money? Redistribution of wealth just doesn't work. When you rob rich people and make life harder for them, poor people are the ones who will suffer the most. In 2008, neophyte New York Governor David Paterson learned this the hard way. New York collected $72 million of taxes from its 20 largest taxpayers in the first three weeks of March 2008, down from $533 million in the same period last year. Paterson, a Democrat, explained this in a speech to the Association For A Better New York.[3] Hypocritical Democrats depend on these top taxpayers to foot the government's bill, yet crusade against them for being successful. These 20 taxpayers left a significant gap in revenue. It would take millions of other taxpayers to fill the gap that they left. Democrats need to realize that without wealthy people this country would die. Wealthy people (not poor people), create jobs, invest in innovation, and make things that improve our lives. They create foundations that sick groups and nonprofit organizations depend upon for financial support. When they have to tighten the belt, it sends shock waves through the economy much different than when a person in the lowest tax bracket loses their job.

Government redistribution of wealth is real institutional discrimination! This is a corrupt concept that I just don't understand. Does elected office give one the authority to take from others what they have earned only to give it to someone else? What criterion is used to decide how much fruit a person gets to keep as a result of their labor and investment? When you consider the ever constant corruption in government, how can one trust that politicians will be honest stewards with the fruits of someone else's labor? I don't believe that elected office gives a person any authority to take away from other people just because they have more than others. What if I feel that the people they are giving my money to don't deserve it? What incentive is there for me to be a productive, taxpaying citizen, if my government tells me that they're just going to take my money away? As I make more, they want increasingly larger portions of it. Furthermore, for a party that promotes equality and fairness, I find it troublesome that they seem to believe that they have been endowed with a special moral authority which forces citizens to believe that they will govern "fairly." "Fair" is a totally subjective term and always subject to corruption. The only way to be fair is to have as little government intervention as possible. To have true equality, everyone should be taxed at the same rate. Successful people shouldn't be penalized with additional taxes. The person that earns $30,000 a year would share the same burden as someone that makes $30 million a year. The goal should be equal protection under the law and not seeking some unattainable societal equilibrium based on liberal values using government powers to take from one, to balance out the other. This is not the role of our government.

Let's just face it, human beings are selfish. It's no different than how children interact with each other. We are born wanting to have things our way. This realization is understood in the essence of capitalism. This doesn't change when you grow up and this is also why communism and socialism always fails. In every case the ones who have been trusted to distribute the resources "fairly" have always kept a little bit more for themselves, their family, and their supporters. The Democrats will try to persuade you with buzz words like "change" and "fair" because of the feelings they conjure. In a practical sense these words cannot be clearly defined just like "rich" and "poor." Yet they use them prominently to pull at the heart strings of the unsophisticated in the electorate.

For instance when President Obama signed into law the Lilly Ledbetter Fair Pay Act of 2009 he said that it was "a simple fix to ensure fundamental fairness to American workers."[4] The legislation cancels out a 2008 Supreme Court ruling that declared plaintiffs had to file wage claims within 180 days of a company's decision to pay a worker less than a counterpart doing the same work. The stated motivation behind the legislation was that Lilly Ledbetter had discovered that for nearly two decades she was paid less her male colleagues for doing the very same work. It claims that over the course of her career, she lost more than $200,000 in salary, and even more in pension and Social Security benefits.[5] The legislation only looks at the surface and doesn't look at the details which may include her performance evaluations through the years, her ability to produce in

20

comparison to her colleagues and other issues such as the company financial conditions at the times of her raises. It only assumes that because she was a woman, she was discriminated against. This is typical liberal shortsighted reasoning. Obama's call for "fundamental fairness" doesn't take into effect the conditions that each worker presents. He only strips away our uniqueness. As a former private sector manager, something Obama wouldn't know about, I know that pay is a personal matter and it differs for each person based on experience, ability, education and productivity. Just because people have the "same job" doesn't mean they deserve the exact same compensation.

Liberalism = Player Hating

You can argue that the entire basis of communism was born in what we call in the black community "player hating," which is a cardinal sin. "Player hating" is when someone has jealousy towards someone else because they have something that they want. Instead of doing what they have to do to get it for themselves, the "hater" harbors feelings of animosity and all too often, plot to take their property. No one respects a "hater." Player hating is the basis of liberalism and it provides the fuel that the agenda driven thought leaders provide to their followers to fan the flames of discontent instead of empowerment. Karl Marx warned the bourgeoisie (the ruling class) that "proletariat" (the workers) would grow tired of their position in society and take over the government. Once they banish the bourgeoisie, they will then rule "fairly." What happens when the working-class takeover of the government? Those people who were once at the bottom are now at the top, new leaders emerge, and then they become the very people they ousted.

"The theory of the Communism may be summed up in the single sentence: Abolition of private property."
–Karl Marx

"From each, according to his ability; to each, according to his needs."
–Karl Marx

"I worked at a factory owned by Germans, at coal pits owned by Frenchmen, and at a chemical plant owned by Belgians. There I discovered something about capitalists. They are all alike, whatever the nationality. All they wanted from me was the most work for the least money that kept me alive. So I became a communist."
–Nikita Khrushchev

"Let the ruling classes tremble at a Communist revolution. The proletarians have nothing to lose but their chains. Working men of all countries, unite!"
–Karl Marx

If you listen to the words of these Communists thought leaders you can hear all of the hate and jealousy towards people who have more than they do. They stir up fear and resentment then basically convince people with weaker minds to trust that they know best. This is the same angst Andrew Jackson tapped into when reuniting the modern Democratic Party in 1828 by taking advantage of the people's trust by manipulating them to perform an agenda which ultimately resulted in only the leaders seizing power that was once in the hands of others. This is no different than today's Democratic National Committee. Instead of working and sacrificing within the system to get what the bourgeoisie has, they plot to manipulate others so that they can take the easy route and commandeer it. The truth is, unless they learn how to earn power in the first place, they will just end up losing it because they have never acquired the knowledge to maintain it. It's like the old saying "easy come, easy go." You can argue that a capitalistic society is also unfair and has its flaws. Personally, I would rather live in a system that allows my hard work, education, sacrifice, and desire to dictate my outcomes instead of some bureaucrat deciding what's best for me. I don't need a politically motivated bureaucrat telling me that I have become too successful and make too much money.

These radically leftist comments are not much different than the modern day Democratic Party and its rhetoric. This economic model discourages the creativity and entrepreneurial spirit that has built our country. This is what sets us apart from the rest of the world and made the United States a leader in a relatively short time. It also provides a disincentive to achieve, when you know that the government will strive to penalize your productivity through heavy taxation and burdensome regulation. Overzealous politicians will use their authority to crusade against people and industries purely for political gain. The thought of some bureaucrat who has been empowered by the law to take from you is almost like organized crime. How is this any different from when mob bosses charged store owners for protection? The Democratic Party has imposed penalties on success. It frightens me every time I hear the Democratic Party's talk about taxing the "rich." What type of inspiration does that give a child to work hard and be successful?

President Barack Obama's White House chief of staff, Rahm Emanuel, spent some time being honest talking about their administration's true intentions of taking advantage of people's difficulties during the economic crisis. Democrats like them salivate when people starve and are unemployed. Emmanuel knows that prosperity doesn't provide the atmosphere for implementing their liberal agenda. That's why the Obama team appears to be excited to see unemployment and foreclosures rise. In an interview with the Wall Street Journal conference of top corporate chief executives before they took office he said "You never want a serious crisis to go to waste." He continued:

"Things that we had postponed for too long, that were long-term, are now immediate and must be dealt with. This crisis provides the opportunity for us to do things that you could not do before."[6]

Many of their friends in the media position them as compassionate, but in reality they see hunger and poverty as an opportunity to gain a captive and loyal audience. These unsuspecting people give the power hungry liberals the chance to force their extreme agenda on the country. In front of The Wall Street Journal's CEO Council, Emanuel stressed that Obama would take advantage of the economic crisis to push universal health care, tax reform, financial re-regulation and energy. In true Democrat style, he pandered to the audience he stood before, refusing to discuss their previous promises to the unions in front of these business leaders. He talked about fairy tales like the "green infrastructure" and promising to give away taxpayer dollars on a major economic stimulus. [7]

They have also encouraged mediocrity and foster low expectations. These elitist party leaders don't seem to care about the messages they send to children, who are raised in an environment seeing poverty. Barack Obama is always talking about hope, but he doesn't give children living in poverty any hope of being successful. Many urban children have been taught that making money defines success. However, when you decode the rhetoric he says that these children might as well stay poor because if you try to be rich, one day he and his Democrat friends are going to do their best to take as much of your earnings away as possible, reinforcing the idea that success is reserved for the privileged which doesn't include them. This is the polar opposite of the conservative belief that success is reserved for those willing to earn it.

It seems that they are proud to create a dependent class of people who become permanent supporters solely for their political gain. It doesn't seem to bother the Democrats that so many of their supporters don't have a clue about their agenda nor are willing to research it. The DNC doesn't mind as long as they continue to enable them through their votes. They have won countless elections because of the generations of government dependents they have created. Congratulations Democratic Party, you have created a class of people with no ambition! You have smothered the American dream with American complacency.

The Model Used By the Modern Democratic Party

They have created a political plantation modeled after the Hermitage, a slave plantation that their standard bearer Andrew Jackson proudly operated. The Hermitage was a 1,050 acre self-sufficient farm where Jackson's slaves performed the hard labor. In 1804 Jackson owned 9 slaves, by 1829 over 100, and at the time of his death in 1845 approximately 150 slaves lived and worked on the property. Jackson set the standard for how his Democratic predecessors should operate the political plantation in the same manner as how he operated the Hermitage. While Jackson cared for his slaves as evidenced by adequate food, housing, some material possessions and the ability of the slave women to reproduce, these people were still in bondage. Slavery was a brutal and cruel system. Jackson taught his Democrats to give slaves just enough to survive, and enough freedom to keep them occupied, but always make them aware that any insubordination will be met with severe consequences. The proud Democrat Jackson taught his predecessors to be relentless when it came to punishment. In a case of a runaway slave, Jackson offered a $50 reward for his capture. He also offered a $10 bonus for every hundred lashes the slave was given up to 300 lashes. For severe offenses, he permitted slaves to be whipped and posted runaway notices.[8] Jackson would be proud to know that his contemporary Democrats show the same level of tenacity when reprimanding African Americans who reject them. We will discuss this throughout the book.

This book presents the observations of a former political slave and explains how one black man has escaped the clutches of the Democratic Party and has decided to be a contemporary Harriet Tubman by forming a new Underground Railroad and returning to the plantation in order to help to free the minds of his people.

2

WHO IS ANDRE HARPER?

For me, growing up in South Florida during the 1980's and 1990's was a unique experience. I lived through what many may consider the end of the old South which has made way for the multicultural society that we live in today. On November 18, 1976 in West Palm Beach, Florida Kelley Lewis gave birth to a baby boy. She was a sixteen year old high school sophomore. According to President Obama, she made a mistake and was punished with a baby.[9] She was a good student that came from a God fearing family. She lived with her father, mother and half brother. My grandfather worked at a local Buick Dealership as a driver and my grandmother was a child care provider. My parents never married and were never together as a couple at any point after my birth.

My grandfather comes from a family of devout Christians. He was the 4th oldest child (of eight) to Bishop Felix Early Lewis and Bishop Helen E. Lewis. He was born in Nashville, Tennessee. His grandmother and my great, great grandmother, Mary Magdalena Lewis-Tate (1871-1930), was the First Chief Overseer and Mother in true Holiness. She established the Church of the Living God, the Pillar and Ground of the Truth in 1903. St. Mary Magdalena felt moved by the Holy Ghost to go out into the world and preach the Gospel, first at Steel Springs, Tennessee. She chose as her co-laborers in the Gospel, her two little sons, the elder one, Walter Curtis Lewis, and the younger one, Felix Early Lewis. In Paris, Tennessee; Paducah, Kentucky; Brooklyn, Illinois; Greenville, Alabama, and throughout many other cities and states in the United States, St. Mary Magdalena stood up and boldly preached the Gospel in the cleanness of the Word of God of things pertaining to the Kingdom of God. [10]

I am very proud of my religious background because the lessons learned allow me to be comfortable in my skin despite the scrutiny that comes from the world. At times I have been made fun of and insulted by members of other Christian faiths because of their misconceptions and haughtiness towards those who practice Holiness. Perhaps these conclusions come from our doctrine's strict rules that govern how a Christian should behave in the world. I'm proud to say that my Holiness upbringing prevented me from drinking alcohol, smoking cigarettes, and doing drugs. Not saying that I didn't have other vices, I just didn't have those. Unfortunately, for my mother, pregnancy before wedlock is frowned upon. However, abortion is looked upon as even worse.

My grandmother came from an entirely different background than that of my grandfather. She was raised in Charleston, South Carolina. Her father was a bootlegger and ran a night spot which was then called a juke joint. She and her twin brother were the youngest of a large brood. My grandmother died in 1993 during my 10th grade year of high school but I have fond memories of her growing up. Some of my fondest memories come from the times she would tell me about her childhood.

My grandmother was a proud Geechee. The Geechees (or Gullah) are Black people who live in the coastal regions of South Carolina and Georgia, which includes the Sea Islands. The Geechees are known for preserving more of their African cultural heritage than any other African American community in the United States. Although they spoke English, the tones and accents contain significant influences directly from West and Central African cultures. The Geechee people have been able to preserve so much of their African cultural heritage because of geography, climate, and patterns of importation of enslaved Africans. African farmers from the "Rice Coast" brought the skills for cultivation and tidal irrigation that made rice one of the most successful industries in early America. This is probably why we ate rice everyday. [11]

Her family infrequently went to church. Several were alcoholics and they had parties all the time and for every occasion. They had parties for every holiday, for when people were born, when people died, going into jail, and getting out of jail. It didn't take much for the family to find a reason to celebrate. However, none of these celebrations were for graduations. When I graduated high school in 1995, I joined a short list of family members that graduated high school, and when I graduated college in 2003, I joined an even shorter list.

For many black children like me, having children early and dropping out of school was clearly the expectation in this part of my family. In fact, when you don't do these things you tend to get ridiculed. Although my family has always been supportive and shown me a great deal of love, I did get picked on for doing well in school. The norm for this segment of my family is to have children early (and often), do some time in jail, and eventually grow tired of the life and get a job. This is no different than many other black families.

My father was considered the brightest and the hope of the Harper family. He too came from a large brood. He was born in the middle of 13 siblings. My grandfather had children from my paternal grandmother and other children from other women. He died when I was five so I don't remember him but he was said to be a strong man that was hard on his children. Although he was caring, he taught his kids to be tough so they were, in turn, hard on each other. My dad told me that there were always confrontations in the household.

My father was a model student. He was the president of his class, scholar, and a star athlete (basketball and baseball). Despite being small, he was tough and people knew not to mess with him. He was also stunningly handsome and possessed the charm to match. His charisma made up for his empty pockets. To this day I still meet women who tell me stories about when they were my dad's girlfriend. Unfortunately for me, the gift for the ladies wasn't one of the many traits passed on to me.

His magnetism is nothing short of legendary. My mother was young and naïve and by all accounts powerless to his appeal. Even in her last days she would always ask if I had heard from him and wanted to know how he was doing. I believe that she never fell out of love with him. She loved him more than I ever would. I don't know very much about their early relationship besides the fact that she got pregnant with me.

My father went on to graduate from Morehouse College. I don't remember meeting him until I was five years old. He may tell you that he was there before then and this may be true, I just don't remember it. By this time I was fully my mother's son. I had inherited her fears which included a fear of water. I was the only boy in a group of children cared for by my grandmother so my natural male instincts of aggression were not apparent at the time.

To my father's credit, this began a string of close to eight years where he would have a strong presence in my life. I can honestly say that those years would help shape the man that I have become, but he left me after that. I can't give him full credit because he didn't complete the job.

By this time my father got married and moved to Los Angeles. I was living with my mother in West Palm Beach in the Dunbar Village housing project. Dunbar gained worldwide attention in the summer of 2007 when a woman was raped, robbed and beaten by several armed intruders in her home. During the incident, her juvenile son was assaulted and forced to perform sexual acts on his mother. [12]

Living in Dunbar was tough then, but over time it has gotten worse. Back then there were a lot of fights and break-ins but I can honestly say that we got along with everyone and did not have many problems while we were there. I did have a few scuffles but that's to be expected when boys are growing up. However, living in the projects should provide motivation to want to do whatever it takes not to have to live in the projects.

Ironically, I lived in one of the worse housing projects in Palm Beach County, yet I went to arguably the whitest public elementary school. My mother worked as a teacher's aide at Belvedere elementary so I ended up attending school there in first grade instead of Roosevelt elementary where I had attended kindergarten and the rest of my elementary years. I went from attending an all-black school to where I was one of a handful of black students. After a year at Belvedere, I began to do what many people in the black community call "talking white." I suppose this means that I try to use proper English.

By now my speaking had changed and my boy instincts were dormant. This infuriated my father so he decided that I needed his form of boot camp. At the end of first grade, I was off to Los Angeles to get a "Hollywood" makeover, which resulted in permanent life changes.

At this point I can honestly say I didn't know my father. I only saw him periodically. Since the few interactions I had with him were enjoyable, I expected that this trip to California would be the same. Boy was I wrong. At this point in my life I still would often wet the bed. My mother and grandmother would just clean up after me which gave me no motivation to do otherwise. So like most people who are not forced to do something, I didn't. That didn't fly at my father's house.

I remember the first time I wet the bed; he beat the crap out of me. That was also the first of many butt whippings that I would endure that summer. He called these beatings "reminders." I suppose that was the perfect name for a method that tormented my psyche during my adolescence and still gives me chills whenever I hear the word being used today. Needless to say, I made a conscious effort to hold it in until I got to the bathroom. I even went when I didn't have to, just to be on safe side. It was worth it because when my father beat me, it was like I could hear thunder crack because he hit me so hard. Next, he tackled my fear of water. I remember being tossed in the pool and given two options. You can guess what they are. Somehow I made it back to the wall. He would also submerge my head under the water in the bathtub. I remember screaming and yelling although the water was never that deep. I was never in any danger of drowning. Eventually, I overcame my fear of water that summer and became a decent swimmer after I returned to Florida.

I remember hating my father as a kid because he used to randomly smack me across the back of my head. I suppose he wanted me to be tough but man it used to hurt. I suppose he wanted me to build a tolerance for pain because I was asking for trouble if I gave him any clue that those smacks hurt. I would do my best to keep it to myself. Anticipating these random smacking made me a nervous wreck. I had a terrible habit of biting my nails as a child. It took me years of confidence building and mental awareness to break the habit.

He eventually moved back to West Palm Beach with his wife Gail who I developed a strong bond with. They divorced in 1990 but Gail and I still remain close. They lived in West Palm Beach from second to sixth grade. I would spend time between both my parents. My father ended up moving to Atlanta, Georgia. I lived with him for most of seventh grade attending Sister Clara Mohammed, a private Muslim school where I learned about the Islamic faith. Close to the end of that year my father faced difficulties which resulted in me moving back to West Palm Beach Florida with my mother. I took a Greyhound bus with only the clothes on my back. I even moved with him for a month during 10th grade which resulted in me returning to West Palm Beach again. I would hear from him rarely after that.

This marked the end of any significant relationship with my father. Once I became a teenager, all I saw was that he wasn't there. Teenagers are too selfish to care about why. Like many other black boys, my journey to manhood would have to be done without my father. I give him acknowledgment for the things he taught me during those years but he didn't finish the job so I can only give him partial credit. My life exposed me to many things, most of which I will do my best not to expose my children to until they are much older.

I also had to learn to exist in different worlds. When I was around my grandfather's family I had to watch my mouth and be respectful of our Christian values. When I was around my grandmother's family, I assimilated by not acting as intelligent as I could have. When I was around my father's family I had to be tough and as I got older I had to be comfortable using colorful language. Harper men are tough and macho. Any signs of weakness will make you the object of ridicule. Having to exist in so many worlds exposed me to clean living, educated people, ignorant people, drug addicts, drug dealers, thieves, alcoholics and the list goes on.

The beauty of being exposed to so many of life's ills is that it allowed me to determine exactly what kind of life I wanted for myself. I was fortunate to have the Cosby Show as a young child. The Huxtables were the benchmark I used for what kind of family I wanted. During the 1980's people were making a lot of money in the drug trade and I saw plenty of it. I also saw the other side of it where people were getting killed and killing themselves using the products. I also saw people getting up, going to work everyday and refusing to get involved with illegal activities. I learned that people have choices to make and that there are consequences to every choice.

Learning About Being Black in America

As a Morehouse graduate and strong black man, my father felt that it was important that I was exposed to what it was like being a black man in America. He also instilled in me distrust of all white people based on our history in this country. I'll be the first to admit that things are much better for blacks now than any other point in history, but I will never forget from whence I came. I was taught about slavery, the middle passage and Jim Crow. Collectively, I call them the Black Holocaust. As a youngster I was taught how slavery affects black people today. Yet, we possess tools to overcome these seemingly insurmountable odds. I also was taught that there are many black people who benefit from black people not learning about their history. Booker T. Washington warned us that:

"There is another class of colored people who make a business of keeping the troubles, the wrongs, and the hardships of the Negro race before the public. Having learned that they are able to make a living out of their troubles, they have grown into the settled habit of advertising their wrongs—partly because they want sympathy and partly because it pays. Some of these people do not want the Negro to lose his grievances, because they do not want to lose their jobs... There is a certain class of race-problem solvers who do not want the patient to get well, because as long as the disease holds out they have not only an easy means of making a living, but also an easy medium through which to make themselves prominent before the public."

This perfectly summarizes the race industry in the United States.

Throughout slavery, we proved that not only can we meet the physical demands placed upon us by our captors, we had the will to persevere thorough the generations of mental torture. We withstood so much mental anguish. Our women were raped, families were separated for profit, plus we had to deal with internal spies who would act as the surrogates of the master. Despite all of this, black people in America have met these challenges head on. Slaves planned, plotted and ran away. Although there were few places to go, many never stopped trying. They held on to hope that one day their children would not have to deal with the same. They stayed alive and dealt with the torture so that one day I may have a chance to get an education and do something positive with my life. They never got a chance to.

It amazed me when I studied and learned about the will of the African-American experience. Democrats have passed and repealed so many laws to make life for us hell (i.e. Jim Crow, The Kansas-Nebraska Act, etc.), yet my people stood with dignity. Despite Democrat oppression through the legal system and otherwise, my people have started universities, learned to read, and climbed Mount Everest. Any of our contemporary collective "struggles" is no comparison to the real struggles of our forefathers. Today black people make excuses as if we're living in 1900.

During my freshman year of high school I attended Suncoast Community High School, where I was a part of the International Baccalaureate Program. The IB program is for serious students only. My middle school teachers recommended me for the program because I had done well but in hindsight I wasn't prepared for the curriculum. By the end of the 9th grade, I had a 1.7 GPA. In 10th grade, I transferred to Palm Beach Lakes High School. Unlike Suncoast, there were no requirements to get into the school. Lakes (as we call it) was a melting pot to say the least. We had our share of clowns, scholars, ignorant folks, white folks, black folks, people from the Caribbean, and a whole lot of hood rats (a derogatory name for street dwellers.) At the end of 10th grade I maintained my 1.7 GPA, and had no clue what I would do with my future. I wasn't a bad kid, I just lacked direction and motivation.

Turning Point

The school's career counselor, Margaret Toombs, knew both my parents when they attended Twin Lakes High School (the predecessor to Palm Beach Lakes high school) and knew that I was not living up to my potential. She took me under her wing and got me a scholarship to attend the Black Male College

41

Explorers Program at Florida A&M University in Tallahassee, Florida. Mr. Thomas Mitchell founded the program to expose black boys, who are headed down the wrong path, to college life. I consider this experience to be the turning point of my life. This is a great example of how people, not government bureaucrats, come together to help improve our local communities.

The Black Male program allowed me to meet boys from around the country. Some had been in trouble with the law and others came from conditions that were much worse than my own. It made me appreciate that I had come and allowed me to me see just how deep the effects of slavery are ingrained in our thought process and how we look at ourselves and each other. Spending time at FAMU, a historically black college, allowed me to see black people who were successful, driven and making positive contributions to the world. Going to college was something that was always distant. No one had really emphasized the importance of a college education because many of the people who I encountered daily were not college educated (excluding teachers.) Seeing these students provided motivation that I could one day be just like them.

The program had strict rules and there was a lot of structure. Most of us had never had any structure so we naturally rejected it. In hindsight, I believe Mr. Mitchell designed this program knowing that young black men suffer from lack of structure. This in turn has led to us being viewed by society as "uncontrollable" and has resulted in so many of us being incarcerated because we are unable to function in society. There were so many nuances in the program that provided me with a personal code of ethics, awakened the self respect that was dormant, taught me how to carry myself with dignity, and pushed me to excel beyond my potential.

We had to always have our shirts tucked in, wear shirts and ties on Friday, as well as full suits to church on Sunday. I didn't have a suit so my mother took me to Goodwill before I left for the program. I hated that ugly suit but it was all we could afford at the time. This taught me that how you dressed had a lot to do with how you feel about yourself as well as how others perceive you.

He employed college students to serve as mentors (program administrators) who made sure that we got to where we were supposed to go. They also served as role models who would give us "recommendations" for when we behaved well and report when we did not. Each program participant was eligible to receive a $25 stipend on Friday afternoons. Every Friday after class all 100 or so participants and mentors would assemble. If you did what you were supposed to do you would get $25. If you caused trouble and broke rules you may not get anything. Then if you received "recommendations" you could receive more. Mr. Mitchell made sure that everyone's total was announced. This taught me that there are rewards for going above and beyond the call of duty. It also taught me that being average resulted in receiving average results.

In addition to the personal growth I received at the program, I was also granted high school credit which helped me eventually graduate with a 2.1 grade point average. Without those credits, I would not have been able to graduate.

Once I returned to Palm Beach Lakes for 11th grade I was a new young man. I had a great deal of confidence which allowed me to get much better grades. I also became active in my church, school and community. Instead of trying to gain acceptance from kids who were unproductive, I surrounded myself with students who were college-bound. Many of these people are still my closest friends today. In fact, I was the last one in my group of high school friends to graduate college. I have found that a big part of my success comes from surrounding myself with people who have a great deal of self respect and character. These traits are contagious just as negative ones are. It's like they say "birds of a feather, flock together."

Defining Moment

Another one of the defining moments of my life came in the 11th grade. I wanted to run for student council vice president. Although Palm Beach Lakes was a majority African American school, the student council didn't reflect the school's population. At the time I thought it was just because white people wanted to dominate everything. Now I know that this also had a lot to do with black people not caring what was going on. Nonetheless, I felt the need to run for student council vice president on a racial platform. In hindsight, that seems silly but it made a lot of sense to me back then.

I just jumped in the race without even learning about student council or its guidelines. I just wanted to make sure that somebody black was on student council next year. It turns out that there was a GPA minimum of 2.5. At the time I may have had a 1.9 or a 2.0. I was already a fairly popular student known for my sense of humor and volatility. My campaign was starting to gain momentum partly because of the enjoyment I found in grandstanding. Nonetheless, the student council adviser came to my class with the news that I had been disqualified because I didn't meet the academic requirement. I refused to get out of the race.

The debates were looming so I put out an announcement stating that I was going to do something big. Normally, only a few of the school's thousands of students would attend student council debates but in 1994 the gym was packed. I didn't even tell my closest friends what I was going to do. I just guaranteed that it would make history. Only Mrs. Toombs was aware of what I had in store. Our principal, Nate Collins was ready as well. I sat in the front row next to Ms. Toombs, in the packed gymnasium silently watching the speeches made by all the candidates. Although it was April in South Florida, I was wearing black sneakers, black jeans, and a black turtleneck sweater. Throughout the program I would turn around and notice that all eyes were on me. I loved it!

When it came time for the last vice presidential candidate to speak I emerged from the audience walking to the podium kindly taking the microphone from the hand of the sitting president. I uttered the words "I have something to say" then I accidentally knocked over a floor plant. As I reached down to pull the plant up my nervousness made it feel as though it weighed 1000 pounds. By the time I pulled it back up I was in the arms of the principal and assistant principal being escorted out of the gymnasium. All of the students were laughing and chanting my name. Mr. Collins promised me a two-week suspension if I walked back inside. I turned around and followed him to his office. Afterwards, I encouraged students to write in my name. I placed second.

The incident sparked a movement at the school where several black students decided to get involved in school leadership. With the class elections coming next month, we got black students elected to five of the twelve available offices. Sadly, I ran for senior class president only to be defeated once again. I remember crying that day because so many students considered me the leader of the "movement," yet I failed when many of them succeeded. My friends and peers assured me that I had earned their respect. My senior year I was elected homecoming king, finally winning in a school wide election.

This ordeal taught me the importance of standing up for what you believe in and that the leader will be the one who suffers the most while others benefit from their sacrifice. I also learned that it's important to have a purpose and a desired outcome whenever you decide to take risks. So many people like to rebel against the system with no reason for doing so or a desired result for their rebellion, yet so many are willing to accept punishment without purpose. I also learned that it is important to gain knowledge of the rules before engaging in anything.

After barely graduating with a grade point average of 2.1, I decided that I wasn't ready for college, much to the chagrin of many family and friends. Only three people supported my decision - my mother, my great-grandmother, and my cousin. I remember sitting outside of church in February of 1995 asking the Lord what should I do with my life. I didn't want to go to college and I didn't want to stay in West Palm Beach. Suddenly my cousin Aaron walked outside. A voice said to me "Aaron was in the Army, ask him about it." He told me about how I could benefit from military service. Within two weeks I took the oath to protect my country and defend our constitution. This is a decision that I am very proud of.

Military Service

Two weeks after my graduation I found myself in the scorching summer heat of Fort Jackson, South Carolina. I picked the three worst months to go to basic combat training. It didn't take long for me to realize that I didn't belong in the military but it was too late. I completed my basic training and went to Quartermaster School at Fort Lee, Virginia to learn about my job as a cook. The guy at the Military Entrance Processing Station (MEPS) who helped me pick a military specialty told me that if you become a cook you will always be able to get a job. He was right, but he didn't say that it would be a good job. I then went to

Ft. Sam Houston (Texas) to complete my training as a diet technician.

After all of my training, I was stationed at Fort Polk, Louisiana, recognized by many as the second worst post in the Army behind Fort Drum, New York. Fort Polk is in the middle of nowhere, far from New Orleans, far from Houston, and far from civilization. While there I was assigned to the 115th field hospital. We were deployed to Egypt for some military training exercises. I learned a lot about life and people during my military years. I didn't enjoy it mostly because of where I was and my job. As a cook you work harder and longer than everyone else. You are required to do everything everyone else does plus feed them. As a result, I am not fond of those years. It served as a means to an end.

The one bright spot of my military career was meeting sergeant first class Darrell Marshall. Sergeant Marshall was an amazing man and he taught me a great deal about leadership. He grew up in New Orleans and had a distinct New Orleans accent. Unlike stereotypical military leaders he wasn't loud and possessed an imposing presence. He was a subtle man that knew how to teach people things without them even knowing it. While working at the large dining facility on Ft. Polk's main post, I never quite got along with the noncommissioned officers (NCOs) that only seemed to care about promoting their friends and female subordinates. I was outside of the inner circle despite how much I worked to be accepted. Sergeant Marshall ran the dining facility on the remote northern part the post used to train visiting soldiers. Some of his cooks had to deploy which left him shorthanded. The large dining facility had to lend him five cooks. They ended up sending him the four worst cooks and me. I began to doubt my own ability when I was coupled with those folks.

I was apprehensive about my new assignment because I heard so many bad things about North Fort. It was nearly vacant and filled with old World War II style barracks. Later, I would find that other noncommissioned officers were jealous of Sergeant Marshall because many people outside of the cook community liked him because of his wit, congeniality and commitment to his soldiers. At 19 years old, while spending time under Sergeant Marshall's tutelage I not only became a much better cook but a better person and leader. When I made mistakes, instead of standing over me and yelling (like the NCO's from the main post) he would say things like "Harper, if I was doing that, I'd probably do it this way" or "you know, if that were me I'd probably try this." During my year with Sergeant Marshall I received several awards and grew tremendously. He ended up being reassigned to another military base and I will honestly say that I cried and hated to see him leave. When he left we were all sent back to the main dining facility and I had to endure another year of hell before I got out. Before he left he told me in confidence that they wanted to send five duds to work for him, but the powers that be said that they had to send at least one good one and that good one was me. He also said that I turned out to be much better than what he expected.

Fast Food Manager

In May of 1998, I saved my leave time which allowed me to get out six weeks early. I remember screaming as I drove and saw the "Welcome to Mississippi" sign. I was finally done with my military service. I moved to Atlanta, Georgia because I planned to go to the DeVry Technical School to get a degree in cell phone technology. The DeVry recruiters came to Ft. Polk and put together a package where I would only have to pay $100 a month for schooling. I fault myself for not reading everything clearly. I was in for a big surprise when I reported to class. In the meantime, I was working as an Assistant Manager at Arby's roast beef restaurant. This was the most grueling job that I have ever had. It was much more demanding than my job as a cook in the Army.

My restaurant was located in Dunwoody, one of Atlanta's affluent suburbs. As a manager, I was tasked to convince people who lived in the city to take the MARTA (public transportation) for an hour to work on a minimum wage job. Not an easy task. Keep in mind, when you're dealing with the minimum-wage workers you have to deal with a host of issues which include childcare (or lack thereof), constantly motivating them to keep the job, constantly calling them making sure they come to work, and being very nice to them even when they don't call in or show up because they know that you need them much more than they need you. They also remind you that if you fire them, then the fast food restaurant down the street will hire them on the spot just like I did. This is why I always pay respect to fast food managers and workers every time I interact with them because they are indeed a group of people worthy of respect.

Many of these full time workers are generally people who dropped out of high school or have little desire to excel in life, while others tend to be high school students and college students trying to make a few bucks. Of course this is a generalization and I had some good people on staff that had been there for a considerable amount of time. Unfortunately, they are the exception and not the rule. The turnover of these jobs is incredible so a manager is constantly hiring and firing.

A manager also has to be a great administrator. They must be able to react in a very fast-paced environment where employee conditions change rapidly and you never know what the next customer will bring. Many customers belittle the fast food staff because of common misconceptions. There were many times where I would protect my employee from unruly customers. There were also times that I worked the restaurant alone because of lack of staff. Arby's was a good company to work for. I appreciated the support I got from my store and area managers.

When it was time to go to school, I discovered that DeVry was much more expensive than the recruiter had revealed and that the $100 a month plan was what I would pay after a combination of Pell grants, G.I. Bill, and student loans. This is much more than I anticipated so I decided not to go to school there. At this point, I was stuck in Atlanta at a job where I worked six days a week and 10-12 hours a day. I was also drowning in debt. My mother encouraged me to live life to the fullest. I was getting new clothes, I had a new car, and I had a really nice apartment that had new furniture. I soon learned that my $1200 a month salary could not sustain this lifestyle.

Like many other people who are considered the working poor, I possessed a poverty mentality. I bought what I wanted without thinking of repercussions. I used credit to get the things I wanted without concern of future payment. I figured I'd have the money to pay for the minimum payments and that one day my ship would come in and I would not have to worry about financial matters anymore. I believed that one day I'd have a big lump sum of money to cover all of these expenses and then some. Eventually I had to pay the piper. My lack of vision and self-control resulted in a bankruptcy claim. I filed for a court consolidation of debt.

My social life was nonexistent. My cousin and one of my best friends from high school were students at Morehouse College and Spelman College. I rarely got to hang out with them. At the end of 1998, I decided that it was time to move back home to Florida and it was time to finally return to Florida A&M University. At 22 years old, I became a college freshman.

College was a great experience for me. After all I had been through it was rather easy. I did well making the Dean's list, the honor roll and graduating cum laude. I was involved in many campus activities. I interned for Procter & Gamble, Tyson Foods, and the Florida House of Representatives. I worked with the student newspaper, the student magazine, and I even had my own TV show for two years. Whatever I thought about doing, I did it. FAMU has created an atmosphere where students can get involved and find the things that they are passionate about so that they can discover who they are.

I also worked the entire time that I was in college. I've worked jobs at Wendy's, a youth shelter, Dillard's department store. I was a substitute teacher, a clerk at Circle K (the graveyard shift), and I even washed postal trucks early in the morning before class. Unfortunately during my junior year, my mother, who had been diagnosed with lupus two years prior, suffered a stroke which left her in a coma for months. During her coma, my daughter was born. When my mother emerged from her coma she could no longer speak or hear. As a result, I had to take responsibility for my then 12-year-old sister. My youngest sister was five years old at the time and then moved in with her father. In addition to my responsibilities as a student, I was now raising a middle school student. Needless to say, this is not what I wanted to deal with during my senior year. Despite all of the challenges, I went on to graduate with honors, cared for my sister and daughter as well as making frequent trips to West Palm Beach to care for my mother and her estate. My mother died on October 31, 2007 at the age of 47 after years of a courageous fight against lupus, one week before Election Day in my city council race.

Life isn't fair, but who ever said that it would be?

3

ESCAPING THE PLANTATION

I won't speak for all black people, so I will speak for myself. Early on, I felt like I was obligated to support all Democrats and vowed to never support a Republican. I was led to believe that all Republicans are racist, evil people that only wanted to destroy blacks. Of course no one could ever tell me why this was so, that's just the way that it was.

I would like to think that I have lived "the black experience." I am a second-generation South Floridian. My grandparents moved to West Palm Beach from Tennessee, Georgia, and South Carolina. Although many don't consider Florida to be the deep South because of its location, what most don't realize is that when black people moved to Florida they brought their culture, traditions, and dialect with them.

According to popular culture my experience would make me blacker than Barack Obama and NAACP leader Ben Jealous. Jealous grew up in exclusive Monterey County, California to mixed parents. He graduated from Columbia, received his master's degree from Oxford, and was a Rhodes Scholar. Not exactly what you want to mention when you want street credibility. Me on the other hand, I barely graduated from a public high school, served in the military and got my college education from a public Historically Black University. However, he is a Democrat, and I am not. Therefore, according to many, he may be blacker than me after all.

So I speak from a perspective of someone who has experienced what the frequent town hall panelists like Michael Eric Dyson theorizes about. I was one of the fortunate ones who lived life in American poverty and was able to be delivered from it. I suppose liberals may not like the fact that my life experiences coupled with my black college education won't allow me to buy in to their self-defeating rhetoric.

I know first-hand the power of self determination and what happens when an environment is created that destroys a person's desire to excel. Living in what many may consider a lower class of society and then rising above it enables me to contrast both perspectives and see how they interact. I see how each benefit from the other. I see how industries and political fortunes have been built based on the collective ignorance and the lack of desire to advance. The social service industry and the Democratic Party depend on people (particularly black people) not wanting to fulfill their life's destiny. Democrats depend on people not wanting to get off of public assistance because they will always provide an audience that will never question their motives, research their statements and blindly obey. This is why Obama and the Democrats rolled back welfare reform in the economic stimulus package. In an opinion article in the Wall Street Journal, former U.S. assistant secretary of Health and Human services Benjamin Sasse and former vice chairman of the American Health Information Community Kerry Weems explained how Obama's economic stimulus would undo the Personal Responsibility and Work Opportunity Act under President Bill Clinton signed when he proclaimed it would end "welfare as we know it." [13] That legislation ended the endless checks that existed since 1965, and replaced it with a five year limit as well as work requirements. The new legislation from the House bill that deals with cash assistance to low-income families includes the phrase: "such sums as are necessary." The "such sums" appropriation language designed to leave the door open which will allow the Democrats to be able to come back in and change to laws to fit their agenda which panders to an audience they have trained to be receptive to any message as long as it offers some type of tangible gain that requires little or no effort. Once you start talking about responsibility and obligations they jeopardize losing this audience. Reciting a list of accomplishments won't matter unless it includes the promise of more hand outs.

Then you have the "race hustlers" who deliver the message on the behalf of the Democrats so they can have a source of income first and foremost and then be considered a "community leader." The Democratic Party fortunes will continue to grow as long as black people continue to embrace ignorance because ignorance is bliss. They create an environment so comfortable where there is no desire to seek knowledge of anything else. The most disappointing thing about my realization is that this so called liberal, progressive, "party of the people" is perhaps the biggest racist entity in the history of America because their sole purpose is to gain power by exploiting the "downtrodden" who they claim to serve. Revered Democrat President Franklin Roosevelt said "The test of our progress is not whether we add more to the abundance of those who have much; it is whether we provide enough for those who have too little."[14] In true elitist form he gloated about destroying the will of others so that they will trust him instead of their own devises but more importantly they will obey his direction. Nowhere in the Democrat plan is there a plan to empower, just to provide. Statements like these helped to create the perception that Democrats "care" about people, but they are simply following a template perfected by President Jackson which allows the wealthy and powerful like FDR to take greater control of the government. Once Democrats seize control of the government, they use its power to encroach our lives and wallets.

Nothing Changes in the House of Democrat

So basically, I should thank Democrats for creating an environment that allowed me to realize just how hypocritical and destructive their policies have been to my people. I have dedicated my life to making sure their crimes are addressed and resolved. What do I mean by creating an environment? Well, their racist beginnings started with the founder of the modern-day Democratic Party, President Andrew Jackson, who was determined to make sure that black people remained in slavery. At the time he organized the Democratic Party as the "party of the people". Today the DNC wants you to think that he meant all people when in fact he only meant white men.

It was and still is the party of the white man, not the party of white women, black people, Native Americans, or anyone else. I'll give Andrew Jackson credit because he was a brilliant man. He organized the working class, just like Karl Marx, because it can be argued that they were neglected. Perhaps the elites of the day (the Republican Party had not been founded) were growing distant from people. He seized the opportunity to acquire power in a way that no one had ever done in that country's short history. He saw that there was a desire for people to have more input in their federal government so he mobilized people and convinced them that he knew best. He taught the unsophisticated masses to trust in his leadership and those who he had endorsed. He was the Democrats first demagogue. He taught his followers not to trust anyone but him. That torch has been passed to Obama. This is the same top-down model that the Democrats use today. [15]

Marcus Garvey was absolutely right in his assessment of communism. He described communism as a white man's creation to solve his own political and economic problems, suggesting that the working class take power from the capitalists. Its creators would tap into the angst caused by the economic struggle of the white masses and harness that anger to gain control. It was never intended to help the economic or political condition of blacks but to raise the amount of wealth received by white workers. Garvey stated "it is a dangerous theory of economic and political reformation because it seeks to put government in the hands of an ignorant white mass who have not been able to destroy their natural prejudices toward Negroes and other non-white people." [16] This explains why the labor union and Democrat agendas are intertwined. Both ignore African Americans. Unfortunately many black people complain when being mistreated by these groups that they support yet accuse others (the Republicans) for their shortcomings.

In 2005, leading labor unions were engaged in a battle about reorganization that could have divided their movement. As usual, no matter what the stakes, blacks are always somehow getting the short end of the stick. For instance, Blacks, make up roughly 14 percent of American union workers, yet accounted for more than half -- 168,000 -- of the union jobs lost in 2004.[17] When the Service Employees International Union (SEIU) and the Teamsters announced their intent to leave the AFL-CIO, the national federation of labor organizations, it posed many questions for the black labor members. Personally, I believe that their concerns would have little bearing on the decisions. Steven Pitts, Ph.D., a labor specialist with the Labor Center of the University of California at Berkeley acknowledged that "The biggest concern [for black union members] is what will be the nature of these conflicts in term of reorganizing." He also added that a split could result in losses in maintaining rights and losing political clout. [18] These are always concerns when you depend on someone else to talk for and provide for your well being.

While Garvey was not particularly a big fan of capitalism, he believed that it provided the best opportunity for the black man to be successful in America. He knew that communism as well as the socialism that today's liberal's champion was, is, and will always be detrimental to the existence of black people in America. When talking about this political failure he said "While it may be good for them, it will be a bad thing for the Negroes who will fall under the government of the most ignorant, prejudice class of the white race. The ignorant white man is cruel and prejudice because of his very ignorance. Therefore, you may see how dangerous it would be to place in his hands, by the strength of his numbers, a government dictated and controlled by him. While the capitalistic system is ruthless and bad, it nevertheless gets the Negro a chance for employment competitive with the working classes of white men; for the purpose of extracting profit from labor, irrespective of the color of labor."[19] Garvey understood the innate racism in the hearts of the liberal and socialist white men. He could see through their disingenuous gestures and understood their true intention which is to always keep the black man as the permanent underclass. His wisdom taught us (and we have learned that) this country has suffered under the hands of ignorant Democrats elected based on the strength of the numbers their support of an educated and unsophisticated electorate that they create. He also understood that capitalism allows the black man to compete against the white man in any realm because the capitalistic system's very existence depends on productivity and the color of that productivity is unimportant.

Jesse Jackson Recruited Me into the GOP

Ironically, the beginning of my political emancipation from the Democratic Party started during my sophomore year of college at Florida A&M University while I was heavily active in the Al Gore presidential campaign in 2000. Like many of my peers at FAMU, I was determined not to let those "racist" Republicans get back in the White House. George W. Bush was at the center of the ire of nearly every black person in the nation. Nearly everyone on our campus was mobilized in the effort to make sure the Democrats maintained the White House. Little did

I know that this was the beginning of my personal paradigm shift.

The Reverend Jesse Jackson was arguably the black face of the Al Gore campaign. He crisscrossed the nation in what seemed to be a mission based on his personal conviction to prevent George W. Bush from getting elected president of the United States. He visited Tallahassee on several occasions during the campaign and I was excited to find out every time he came. I made it a point to be as close to him as possible so that I could see him because, up until then, I had always admired Reverend Jackson.

Not only was I fortunate enough to see Reverend Jackson at public events, I was also able to meet him. While in college, I was considered to be a student leader because I was very active in student organizations and activities. I suppose you could say that I was a member of Dubois's talented tenth based on those credentials. Nonetheless, my designation as a "student leader" afforded me the opportunity to meet Reverend Jackson in a closed meeting in our student government chamber. I was handpicked to listen to what Reverend Jackson had to say. Because everyone wasn't invited to this meeting I just knew that the topics discussed had to be of the utmost importance and I was honored to be selected to take part, although I had no clue what was going to be discussed.

When I arrived in the chamber I noticed other students who were also considered "student leaders" so I knew this had to be important. I didn't realize this at the time, but this is what happens in many of our nation's African-American communities. The so-called "leaders" are handpicked to dictate to the other members of the community who and what they will support. These handpicked leaders are generally members of the elite families, the prominent ministers, the business owners, etc. While not impossible, it's generally difficult for a person outside of these boundaries to establish themselves as a leader amongst this group. It starts from meetings just like the one I was attending in school. They then evolve into back room political dealings which determine who is going to get elected, who is getting the new development deal, who is getting the next big appointment, and most importantly it identifies which members of the community that will NOT benefit from the deals. More often than not, these meetings result in arguing over the scraps the white man tosses off of his plate.

Once we were all assembled Reverend Jackson began to make his remarks. He began by stressing the importance of this election. He talked about the repercussions of a failed effort to get Al Gore elected president. He stated that we had to do everything we could, and in fact every vote was important. He mentioned how important Florida was in achieving victory. He obviously had been briefed on how close the election would be. This made his job critical, making him that much more valuable. I can personally say that I didn't think it was going to be as close as he made it out to be. In hindsight I realized why he traveled to Florida so much. He then talked about the tyranny of Governor Jeb Bush and made us livid. Of course he knew what he was doing. We were baited into his rhetoric. Our emotions had taken over our logic and like rabid wolverines, we were ready to fight. He then began to accuse George W. Bush of heinous racially motivated crimes while he was governor of Texas, not hesitating to accuse him of being racist and blatantly race baiting. I thought he was being completely honest because a "man of God" such as he could do no less. However, it just didn't seem right that a man so blatantly evil could even make it to a position to run for president.

Jackson's absurdity made me question his motives and what I was being told. This moment of objective thinking without loyalty to the Democrats was the beginning of my political emancipation. Why was this "man of God" spending so much time vilifying another, instead of talking about the merits of his candidate? Nothing in the conversation mentioned Al Gore's policy platform or his credentials. Things just weren't adding up. My holiness background taught me that the mission of a clergyman was to save souls but Reverend Jackson didn't seem to be interested in saving the souls of the Bush's or even ours for that matter, so he must have had another goal, but what?

While everyone else seemed to really be getting wrapped into the emotions of the moment, I began to feel uneasy. I considered myself a fairly and reasonably educated young man at the time and not stupid by any means. I was paying a lot for my college education, putting myself through school only using my G.I. Bill, loans and money I earned working after class. I took my education seriously and didn't appreciate someone coming onto my campus and addressing me in such a condescending manner. I don't care who you are. I expected more intelligent conversation and perhaps some strategy on how we were going to defeat the Republicans using principles and ideas. I got nothing of the sort.

What I did get was some of the most racist, insulting, and emotionally charged rhetoric I have ever heard. When he said "stay out of the bushes" and went on to say that if George W. Bush gets elected he will make sure that black people become slaves again, I began to realize that my service to Al Gore and the Democratic Party was over! I refused to put up with any more of these types of insults to my intelligence. While others seem to be impressed, I was furious. I began to question this entire campaign and why I was supporting these people to begin with. Why would they send such an inarticulate surrogate to a college of 13,000 young intelligent African Americans speaking such nonsense? The answer is that they consider him among the best blacks have to offer which means they consider the rest of us beneath him. I had never been so insulted in my entire life. The worst part about this was that one of our "heroes" was being used as an insignificant lackey. We look up to Jesse. You will find his profile hanging up on many black history displays in community centers across the country. We are taught that he is a hero. His goal was to sway and then herd our votes and minds. I realized that the purpose of this meeting was for us to become Jesse's surrogates in Tallahassee after he had gone. There was no way I would do any more campaigning for Al Gore or any other Democrat.

Many people have asked me why I get so angry with the Democrats instead of Jesse Jackson. I realized that a much larger entity directed Jackson to persuade black students to work hard. On a larger scale, Rev. Jackson was simply a pawn. I don't see anything to gain by addressing my grievances with the messenger.

Challenging My Indoctrination

After I decided to end my work in the Gore campaign, I went on with my life and even though I no longer participated in his campaign, I vaguely recall voting for him (something that I'm not very proud of.) However, I did take his money on Election Day as some level of vindication by getting as many of my friends to get money by holding signs of the corners. Most of them just showed up at the end of the night to collect checks. Living in Tallahassee allowed me to watch the aftermath of the 2000 election up close. I watched what many people like to consider the Republicans stealing the election. But that's just not true. What I saw was the Democrats getting their butts whipped from coast to coast and pulled out every trick in the book to legislate the victory. They acted like sore losers (a common occurrence and a typical scenario after a Democrat defeat) just like they did in 2004. They seem to always scream foul after defeat. For some reason, they didn't complain about voting irregularities after the 2006 midterm elections or in 2008 when ACORN helped to hand them large congressional majorities.

They then began to talk about voter irregularities and voter intimidation. They made it seem as though Republicans had deployed ruffians who stood guard in front of every precinct with guns and batons while waiting to knock the blocks off of any minorities who came to exercise their constitutional right. I was in Tallahassee along with several hundred fellow students; we were all on guard to make sure that nothing like this would happen. Of course after the election, Democrats and so-called "civil rights leaders" made serious accusations that voter intimidation was widespread. Given the hostile climate, any credible incidents would have been front page news. According to them, this happened in many places, yet there were no credible documented incidents to support their claims.[20]

Nonetheless, what bothered me the most is that Jesse Jackson never bothered to tell us that he was campaigning for Al Gore and being paid by the Democratic Party! He came under the guise of a concerned minister and African-American community leader. He acted as though his primary reason for being in Tallahassee was to prevent a racist regime from taking office. Of course he didn't wear his Democratic hat; he delivered his message wearing his minister hat as he seems to do most often. [21]

Now don't get me wrong, I am not against ministers or so-called African American community leaders campaigning for their favorite candidates, or the ones who pay the most (in most cases); what I am against is so-called leaders blurring the lines of their capacities and thus fooling the masses into believing their intentions are righteous. I have campaigned for several Republican candidates including myself since I left the Democratic political plantation in 2000, and many in Cincinnati considered me a community leader.

I have always taken the designation of a leader within my community seriously. That means that people trust, respect, and want to know your opinions about various issues. Many seek your counsel and many times depend on what it is that you say. Given this responsibility by my peers I believe that it is important not to betray their trust in order to advance my individual political beliefs and affiliation. I believe that I have a solemn duty not to wear my political hat when I'm being sought to provide leadership and counsel to members of my community. It is important for me to offer unbiased solutions when I am in a community leader capacity which includes speaking to impressionable youth and civic groups in non-political forums.

I find it incredibly hypocritical and unscrupulous when community leaders are being paid (or compensated in some way) to campaign on the behalf of a candidate or issue and neglect to inform the masses of their compensation. I am not against a man making a living but the man should be honest to the people who trust and support his opinion. I believe that it's even more imperative for any minister to inform people of his compensation regardless if it's monetary or someone assurances of some type of appointment because not only is he blurring the lines of his community leader capacity he is now blending his spiritual obligations with his personal allegiances. He should make it known that he is speaking for himself and not as the head of the church.

Contemporary black people don't know anything about real voter intimidation like our brothers and sisters in Zimbabwe. President Robert Mugabe let it be known that there are severe consequences to anyone who opposed his reelection. While Zimbabweans are accustomed to violence, the beatings and bloodshed have been epidemic since after opposition candidate Morgan Tsvangirai pushed longtime President Robert Mugabe into a runoff election for the nation's top post. When the violence became unbearable Tsvangirai dropped out of the race, citing intimidation and vote-rigging and went into hiding at the Dutch Embassy, while the violence continued. Mugabe seemed unfazed when he heard accounts of the rapes and maiming being reported across the country, people having their hands chopped off, fingers broken, etc. His zealous supporters were willing to do anything to make sure their candidate captures the office. [22]

They remind me of the zealous Obama supporters. In Ohio, Sen. Hillary Clinton, said that she had received reports from the field of Obama poll workers being kicked out of precincts for aggressively challenging voters. [23] Adding it up, she said, "and it's a pattern." Democrat Secretary of State Jennifer Brunner has rebuked Sen. Barack Obama's campaign for trying to staff precincts with poll workers who presented insufficient credentials and said that "It's a pretty sad thing that people we now have to worry about are fellow Democrats," she said. [24] I doubt if Obama supporters would try to cut off any hands but with overzealous liberals, you can never be too sure.

Black preachers are notorious for muddying the waters when it comes to promoting their candidates, especially Democrats. Furthermore, they allow Democrats to insult their flocks with their presence then allow them to talk down to their parishioners by insulting their intelligence with language that they wouldn't dare use in any other forum. I just don't understand how black people continue to allow this. Blacks are always talk about fighting, and "the struggle." We need to start by rejecting and standing up to those in our own communities who keep us down instead of focusing our energy on so many outside forces that have no bearing on our lives. We love to engage in fights and putting ourselves on pedestals by advocating for others and fighting against the government, while we have so many internal issues that need to be addressed. Issues like violence, crime, teenage pregnancy, the proliferation of AIDS in our community and education are issues that we should be handling ourselves instead of petitioning others to remedy. Somehow our leaders seem to ignore this because championing issues like personal responsibility aren't as lucrative as the war in Iraq or presidential politics. It's like the old folks used to say "Sweep around your own front door before you try to sweep around mine." Bill Cosby is correct; our community needs to focus on self-improvement.

It was interesting to watch the Obama-Reverend Wright situation unfold. This gave America a glimpse of what black people have been doing since slavery. The black church has always been the one place where black people can publicly vent their frustration without reprimand from the world. Although Wright preaches black liberation theology which is a smaller segment of black Christianity in America, he does perform like many other black preachers. A lot of black preachers get in front of their parishioners on Sunday and cast judgment on white people and America with reckless abandon. Wright is not alone when he makes statements like America started AIDS to kill blacks, and that America brought September 11th on itself and so forth. He is just the first to have his sermons broadcast across to a mainstream American audience because of his relationship with Obama. He didn't say anything that black people haven't heard in church already. What I find most humorous is that a lot of these Black preachers are firebrand militants on Sunday in front of black people, but the rest of the week, they are humble servants of God in front of everyone else. Wright is only guilty of letting the cat out of the bag. While I don't agree with Wright on many things, I respect him for having the guts to speak his mind and staying true to his beliefs. Despite the pressure he didn't back away from what he thinks to be true.

I am truly a believer in free speech. I don't believe in political correctness nor do I apologize for what I said if I meant to say it. I do realize that there can be consequences to things that are said. Not everyone is as accepting of people's differing opinions as I am. Some people get offended and are willing to become hostile because they can't accept those that don't see things the same way as they do. That's why it is important that if you are willing to make your opinions known, you have to be willing to stand by them. That's why I admire people like Dr. King and Malcolm X. so much. They knew that their lives were at stake when they made statements and were willing to pay the price, unlike many of today's so-called civil rights activists who like to conjure the spirit of Dr. King, then run and hide when the going gets tough. They like to cast judgment on white people then run to the very same white people for police protection when their mouths write checks that their behinds can't cash.

Now that Reverend Wright's feelings towards the United States are known to the world you can imagine that there are certain segments of the population who weren't as accepting as I am to his right to free speech. Certain people would consider his language treason. Black America Web reported that during the 2008 election season leaders of Wright's church, Trinity United Church of Christ, asked reporters for respect, saying threats and a media onslaught were disrupting worship at the South Side church. The church then increased security in response to threatening telephone calls, letters and e-mails. I would imagine that if someone made good on one of those threats then those evil Chicago police officers would be the first ones called. Chicago police monitored the situation but had no reason to believe the congregation or the neighborhood was in danger. [25] What probably happened was they received a few threatening phone and became afraid. The Rev. Otis Moss III, who has replaced Wright, said that some called saying "Wright would meet Jesus sooner than he thinks." I've heard comedian Rickey Smiley make more threatening phone pranks than that. What needs to happen is that people who decide to make their comments known should be willing to stand by them and not run for cover when people don't accept them.

People like Jesse Jackson and Al Sharpton have been making comments like that for years and continue to do so. Their type is nothing new. The phenomenon we know as "community leaders" didn't start in the 1960s or the 1980s. You have to look back much further to find the origins of these hand-picked and/or self-appointed community leaders. Now these people are picked by Democratic Party bosses or the mass media. Malcolm X. eloquently explained this dynamic. He called them "house negroes." [26] They were the hand-picked representatives that the slave masters would choose to be the leader of the slaves. They spoke on behalf of the slave community. However, their primary role was to always be aware of what was going on amongst the slaves and to keep the masters informed. Now the role has been assumed by the so-called civil rights leaders. They create social justice organizations and then give each other achievement awards (where they shake down the private sector for $1000 a table) and we are supposed to admire them for their "fight" for civil rights. Today these people have proven that being a "house negro" can be lucrative, even though the role has remained virtually unchanged since slavery.

In my opinion a "house negro" and "sellout" are synonymous as well as unflattering. You may ask "why would a person want to have this role?" Wouldn't this be undignified? Perhaps it will be difficult for them to look in the mirror knowing that they have sold their soul to their very oppressor. The master knew that he couldn't just designate this person without them receiving some type of compensation. He knew that this person would have to gain something in order act as the eyes and ears of his community. The master also knew that this person would need to gain individual privilege. So he appealed to man's natural ego and greed. This is easy to understand when you realize that the slaves were taught to feel inferior. The master knew that even the insignificant accolades in his eyes would be significant milestones to someone who considered himself as someone else's property. The payment this slave received is comparable to the payment that many of today's hand-picked community leaders receive.

This is how it works. The slave masters, and now the Democratic Party bosses, entice the most talented, best spoken and most respected members of the community with promises of prestige and wealth. They appeal to their ego with compliments and subtle comparisons with other members of the community letting them know that there's "something about them" that makes them better and more capable of becoming the leader than others. During slavery this spokesman was given access to the house and better food than his peers. He got the prestige of being out front and didn't hesitate to flex his muscle when one of the other slaves challenged his authority. He and his family were benefactors of this treatment while the others were doomed to suffer. Today this person can be blatantly compensated with a financial payoff or in most cases fancy appointments or access. In both cases the person was given an official platform in which to address the other members of the community.

The "House Negro" model is still in effect today. The Urban Dictionary has several accurate definitions for "House Negro" also known "House Nigger." Definitions include "A black person that does their best to please white people even if it means disowning their own racial identity." Another definition is "a black person that sucks up to the white man for benefits. From slave times where the house nigga would get to work inside the house as opposed to picking cotton out in the hot sun."[27] They also include a definition meaning "a black Republican" because of the "Southern Strategy," which is no surprise. The first two definitions accurately describe many of today's black leaders who do the bidding of the Democratic Party. These politicians and community leaders get to remain in positions of power and influence as long as they continue to deliver the votes to the Democrats.

When I reflect on my lessons in life, what I was taught and the trials I have been through, I realize that a man has to be strong in order to make it in this world. Liberals and especially race hustlers would like for the world to believe myths like productive black men are on the verge of extinction, black men can't adapt, black men are unemployable and black men are basically unable to function in a civilized society. They want you to believe that black men like me cannot survive without liberal intervention. Slavery was designed to break the spirit of the black man by beating him in front of his family, insulting him, promoting distrust among his peers, etc. Many of these men sacrificed pride and dignity in order to survive while others refused and paid the ultimate price. Men like Marcus Garvey defied the White man and unapologetically proclaimed his pride. Many contemporary black men lack the intestinal fortitude to stand on their own beliefs and speak out against their Democratic masters. They are willing to do or say anything to stay in good standing and win favor with them.

In order to win some points from the climate change liberals, the veteran house Negro Jim Clyburn used his first instinct, which was to cast black people as sympathetic victims regardless how absurd their assertion was. They want you to suspend disbelief so that their comments sound profound when in reality they are absurd. All human beings live on the planet earth and are subject to the same forces of nature. Yet race hustlers like Clyburn took an intellectual leap by insisting that somehow Mother Nature, like everyone else, discriminates against black people. "It is critical our community be an integral and active part of the debate because African-Americans are disproportionately impacted by the effects of climate change economically, socially and through our health and well-being," Clyburn said in front of a group of primarily white people at the National Press Club in Washington, D.C., to help launch the Commission to Engage African-Americans on Climate Change, a project of the Joint Center for Political and Economic Studies. [28] Is this intended to be leadership or inspiration? I call it cowardice!

Barack Obama is perhaps the biggest coward going among the black men in national Democratic leadership. For a guy who excelled in hard nosed Chicago politics, he sure is proving to be a wimp on the national stage, at least when it comes to sticking up for the needs of black people. I must admit that he is a warrior when it comes to defending the liberal agenda. He showed his yellow streak down his back when he declined to engage in debates.[29] After Clinton creamed him in a debate in 2008, he rejected her challenges once he took the lead in the polls. McCain challenged him to travel the country and discuss the issues outside of the conventional moderated debates in intimate town hall settings around concerned citizens instead of his irrationally loyal "fans." While Obama challenged McCain to stick to the issues in front of his rabid fans, his spokespeople sent releases declining any invitation to discuss issues without the assistance of cameras, the teleprompter, the scripts and his liberal friends in the media. As a black man, Obama's cowardice is embarrassing. As president he continues to live the scripted life of a candidate and continues to evolve as a manufactured product while the liberal agenda is rammed down our throats. I was hoping the first black president would have the guts to take on any challenge. Boy was I wrong.

Obama's Vice-President Joe Biden obviously agrees with me. Biden candidly told Democrat big money supporters that there was no doubt in his mind that a crisis will occur during Barack Obama's first six months in office.[30] He, like many world leaders, knows weakness when they see it and they will be eagerly waiting to test his mettle. He went on to tell his supporters that Obama would undoubtedly make the wrong decision and that they should continue to zealously support him and to use their influence to force others do the same. While this may appear to be a call for patience, it's actually a liberal political strategy to buy them some time. He is staying on message and bullying his love struck liberal supporters into staying on board. He basically told them not to scrutinize Obama like liberals scrutinized George W. Bush. They should support their leaders unconditionally without any dissent.

If you pay attention, you'll notice that the Democratic Party, mostly its leaders, acknowledge, perpetuate and bask in their role of continuing slavery in America. Of course it's not as blatant as the chattel slavery that Democrats were willing to die for to preserve in this country, it's much more subtle and sophisticated. In a speech commemorating Dr. Martin Luther King Jr. in 2006, Senator Hillary Clinton made remarks at a black church in Harlem accusing Republican leaders of running the United States House of Representatives "like a plantation." [31] Reading this news article made me conjure thoughts of grade school when we'd say, after being accused of something, "it takes one to know one." In this case, being the masters of slavery as the Democrats are, she knows what a plantation looks like and she can teach the Republicans a thing or two about running a plantation. Last time I checked, Blacks typically vote nine to one Democrat.

The statement derived from the Democrat's frustration in being the minority party in Congress. For years they were unable to pass their liberal legislation in the Republican controlled Congress. According to the rules of the House of Representatives, House leadership can set limits on debate and decide which legislation comes up for a vote. For years Democrats complained about how Republicans have been taking advantage of their majority. This is no new practice, this is what happens in every Congress, and the majority party has always set the agenda. Democrats know this. I find it highly hypocritical that this wasn't an issue during the 40 year reign of the Democratic Party in the house when they had much more power. They didn't complain when Tip O'Neill jousted with Ronald Reagan. And I doubt that the Democrats complain that they have too much power now that they have regained control of the Senate and House in 2006 with the left wing extremist Nancy "wicked witch of the West Coast" Pelosi at the helm.

After these blatantly offensive and racist remarks by Senator Clinton, the Democratic Party's "House Negros" were dispatched to defend her offensive remarks. In one case Reverend Al Sharpton defended her statement by saying "I absolutely defend her saying it because I said it through the 2004 elections," he said. [32] You'll notice that Democrats and their "House Negros," like Sharpton, constantly accuse others of being racist. They can't help it. Racism is their livelihood and its how they remain relevant. They have to keep race top of mind while challenging the rest of us to work towards racial equality. The mission of Al Sharpton's National Action Network is to "promote a modern civil rights agenda that includes one standard of justice and decency for all people regardless of race, social justice for communities, and the improvement of race relations."[33] The mission of the National Association for the Advancement of Colored People is to "ensure the political, educational, social, and economic equality of rights of all persons and to eliminate racial hatred and racial discrimination."[34] These open ended goals are clearly designed to be ambiguous, immeasurable, as well as unattainable which gives them a permanent reason to stay relevant, despite societal shifts and progress. They have to exist in the past while claiming to move forward.

Accusing someone of being a racist is a serious accusation that flows freely from their mouths and one that is nearly impossible to prove. The civil rights activist's inability to move beyond race as the primary source of our society's problems makes them the biggest racists and I will present my case over the course of this book.

4

I AM A REPUBLICAN BECAUSE...

After dissociating myself with the Democratic Party I took some time off from politics. I was still in college enjoying college life and politics just wasn't on the radar screen. However, my experiences from the 2000 election left a bitter taste in my mouth. Becoming a Republican had never crossed my mind because of my inner bigotry towards them that had been implanted in my psyche without me even knowing it. Although I was entirely done with the Democrats, and considered myself a political independent, becoming a Republican was never an option because I didn't want to be considered an "Uncle Tom" or a "sellout" in my community. So to combat any notions of the possibility of being perceived this way by my brothers, I decided to extensively study the political history of both parties in order to understand their principles and beliefs. To do this I had to remove all of the biases that had been implanted in my thought process since birth. I had to remove any loyalties that were there and be totally objective and open to findings that may make me uncomfortable. As a proud black man, I had to see how the histories of these parties affected my experience in this land.

In order to be totally objective I had to remove my contemporary outlook and take a historic and holistic approach to my research. I wanted to connect the dots of the past, present and future in order to have a holistic understanding of the American political system. I am a firm believer that times change but people don't. God made the Ten Commandments over 2000 years ago because man was having issues with murder, larceny and adultery just as they are today. I believe that the same sentiments still run our two political parties even though the names have changed through the years. I have found that unlike many other cultures African-Americans are detached from our own history and know or care little about it. We've been led to believe that the black experience began with the civil rights movement and that, because we were enslaved, we will always be mistreated in this country. That's all the Democrats want us to know about our history because that's all they have on their website in regards to the black experience. This abbreviated outlook of our history allows us to constantly view and promote ourselves as eternal victims. Personally, I believe that it is an abomination for a people that have overcome so much to essentially reject their own history. It is saddening to meet so many black children who don't know what the Middle Passage was. I'm sure a Jewish parent would be disgusted if their child was unaware of their Holocaust and all of the trials and tribulations that they faced as a people.

In addition to books on political theory, I was influenced by books like Up From Slavery by Booker T. Washington, Miseducation of the Negro by Carter Woodson, Message to the

Black Man by the Honorable Elijah Muhammad, the Conscience of a Conservative by Barry Goldwater, Message to the People by Marcus Garvey and of course the Autobiography of Malcolm X. These great men and their recordings served as the foundation of my political and conservative beliefs. If knowledge and understanding of history and politics qualifies me as being a "sellout" in the black community then I'll proudly accept. The lessons given by these men serve as poison to the liberal message of government dependency and it threatens their entire existence. It has been told that the best place to hide something from a black person is by putting it in a book. The Liberals are fully aware of power of knowledge. That is why they invest heavily in the so-called Negro leaders of the civil rights establishment that persistently vilifies the minority of blacks who try and share this knowledge of our past by using groupthink and deceitful tactics that cause the community to mistrust or dismiss black conservatives as tokens of the Republican Party.

Besides the many books and observations, I would have to say that the biggest influence of my political beliefs come from Malcolm X. If I had a chance to meet anyone in history he would be at the top of the list. After President Kennedy was assassinated, Malcolm X. made his infamous "chickens coming home to roost" speech. The tragedy is that history only remembers this one line from this brilliant speech. That line ultimately forced him out of the Nation of Islam, which some would argue was the beginning of the end of his life. However, if you examine the speech you will learn that he made some profound statements contrasting liberal and conservative political beliefs. There is no way that I can properly summarize his genius so this is an entire excerpt:

Let us examine briefly some of the tricky strategy used by white liberals to harness and exploit the political energies of the Negro. The crooked politicians in Washington, D.C., purposely make a big noise over the proposed civil rights legislation. By blowing up the civil rights issue they skillfully add false importance to the Negro civil rights "leaders." Once the image of these Negro civil rights "leaders" has been blown up way beyond its proper proportion, these same Negro civil rights "leaders" are then used by white liberals to influence and control the Negro voters, all for the benefit of the white politicians who pose as liberals, who pose as friends of the Negro.

The white conservatives aren't friends of the Negro either, but they at least don't try to hide it. They are like wolves; they show their teeth in a snarl that keeps the Negro always aware of where he stands with them. But the white liberals are foxes, who also show their teeth to the Negro but pretend that they are smiling. The white liberals are more dangerous than the conservatives; they lure the Negro, and as the Negro runs from the growling wolf, he flees into the open jaws of the "smiling" fox.

The job of the Negro civil rights leader is to make the Negro forget that the wolf and the fox both belong to the (same) family. Both are canines; and no matter which one of them the Negro places his trust in, he never ends up in the White House, but always in the dog house.

The white liberals control the Negro and the Negro vote by controlling the Negro civil rights leaders. As long as they control the Negro civil rights leaders, they can also control and contain the Negro's struggle, and they can control the Negro's so-called revolt. The Negro "revolution" is controlled by these foxy white liberals, by the government itself. But the black revolution is controlled only by God.[35]

Malcolm X. was able to masterfully articulate my political beliefs and mistrust of the civil rights establishment and liberals in this speech. He dealt with the same issues that we are dealing with today. He claimed no political party and was critical of both but especially the liberal because of their deceitful tactics. I found it much easier to exist in the Republican Party because of the transparent nature of conservatives. I am never under the illusion that I am specially favored. Conservatives stick to their principles and that's fine with me. Conservatives believe that this country's blessings and opportunities are available to anyone regardless of their color or gender. They don't practice identity politics that the Democratic Party specializes in. I see blacks being taken advantage of by liberals everyday but especially during election season. We operate as mindless sheep by inflating their poll numbers. Malcolm X. was absolutely correct about those white liberals. By controlling the black leaders, the Democrats control black people, their agenda, their votes, their minds and their lives. These lessons have allowed me to break away from their mental bondage and escape the Democratic Party's plantation!

Although the Democrats no longer received my outward support, they still had control over my thoughts and views towards politics. Breaking the chains of the mind control that were implanted in my thought process was tough to break, even with the lessons I had learned. Since the 1960s, Blacks have been born with an innate loyalty for Democrats and taught to believe that you must hate the Republicans and reject any thoughts that threaten your loyalty. We are taught that Democrat loyalty is part of our ethnic identity even though they have done nothing to deserve it. In fact, Democrats should never receive any black support because of their murderous reign of terror that lives on today. Nonetheless, my liberal indoctrination almost prevented me from great opportunities, but furthermore it almost kept me on their plantation.

After September 11, 2001, I watched a newly elected George W. Bush stand strong in the face of an enemy without a face who had just executed the most heinous act of domestic violence that we had experienced since Pearl Harbor. He showed true leadership during those times and I must admit his bravado made me look at Republicans differently. It's not that I agree with everything he's done since then but given the circumstances faced in his presidency, he did the best that he can do, and I don't think anyone could have done better, especially not Al Gore. President Bush made me reassess my outlook of the Republican Party.

Exploring My Options

In 2002, I saw a flyer for the Florida A&M University College Republicans. In a school of 13,000 intelligent black students, many of which are fiercely loyal supporters of the Democratic Party, there were not people beating down the door trying to join the club. In fact, there were only about five people at the meeting. They were all freshman and I was a senior. They impressed me with their confidence in the party's beliefs, they talked about the history of the party, and didn't give a hard sell. They presented their side and left the decision to join up to me, unlike the Democrats who are pushy and expect blacks to always obey them. Plus the Democrats on campus always seemed to get frustrated when you asked tough questions about their history and policies. Many times they were oblivious to their party history and platform. Other times they probably did know the answer but wouldn't give it because they were having a hard time coming up with a bull crap answer. Honesty is not a policy they seem to hold sacred. Nonetheless, I decided to keep the literature and do some of my own research.

I started by contrasting the histories of both parties and then I contrasted their principles. To say that I was shocked would be an understatement. My sources were direct literature from the Republican National Committee and the Democratic National Committee. I looked at their websites, which gave accounts of the party history from their perspective before I looked at third-party sources. If someone takes the time to do their homework you will find that there is no comparison when it comes to which party has done more for African Americans in the United States. You'll find that the Democrats are not only disingenuous but they omit large time frames as well as pertinent information from their role in shaping our nation. If you didn't know any better you would think nothing important happened during the 50 year time period from the mid-1800s to the early 1900s. Only the Civil War happened, which probably isn't that important since the Democrats have no mention of it in their party's history. [36]

What impressed me the most when I started to do my research was that the Republican Party was the party of principles. From the beginning, the Party believed in individual freedom, patriotism, limiting government, protecting our land,

and despite the contentious political climate of the day, it fought to end slavery. I can't imagine the courage it took for those men to oppose an institution that directly resulted in the early wealth creation of this nation. The abolition of slavery could have potentially destroyed the economy of this country. Nonetheless, they fought to end it anyway because principles trump the situational ethics practiced by Democrats.

You would be naïve to think that they all were righteous men who cared about the well-being of the enslaved Africans. That's not the case, because many of them opposed it for various reasons. Not all of them felt that it was the right thing to do. Regardless the reason, they still did it. The Party came together to fight it. They knew that the Democrats would rather start a new nation or die, than to live in a nation where they would be considered equal to a black man. I am sure that today's liberal Democrats would have the same resolve as their forefathers if blacks all of a sudden left the "hood" and started to move into their liberal enclaves with their green homes and eco-friendly coffee shops. What will happen when blacks abandon their low-income abodes and their Section 8 rental units which liberals reserved just for them? Liberals will show their true intolerance when forced to live beside people they consider below them.

I believe it is important that history recognizes the sacrifices these early Republicans made in making the difficult stand to abolish slavery. The sacrifices were not only political, but many risked their lives and reputations in order to eliminate this barbaric institution that the Democrats wanted to preserve as part of our national fabric at all costs. As we have learned throughout history from the 1800s and 1900's up until the present day, it's not unfathomable for Democrats to resort to violence or underhanded tactics if they don't get their way.

How Liberals Treat Blacks That Don't Obey

During my run for Cincinnati City Council, I was a victim of some of the same shady tactics today's so-called good hearted liberal Democrats used against my ancestors. Unlike my ancestors, Democrats didn't drag me out of my house and burn crosses on my yard. They did however pull up my yard signs sooner than I could put them down. Someone even went through the trouble of collecting them, finding the address of my treasurer (who lived in the suburbs), and piled them in his front yard. I am sure they could have cared less about scaring his wife and children, they just wanted to intimidate us because they feared our message. These cowardly liberals also didn't hesitate to question my sexuality on blogs because I smiled in many of my pictures. It's funny that liberals, who claim to support gay rights, are quick to use gay references as an insult like when the blogger Perez Hilton, who is extra gay, called rapper, Will.i.am, a "f**king f*ggot"[37], which is a synonym for a gay man. He meant it as an insult and not a compliment. I don't consider being gay an insult. If that makes your boat float then that's fine with me. Just don't expect me to sail with you. The good thing about blogs is that they finally give the person who sat in the back of the classroom a forum to say what he never would have the guts to say aloud. Now they can be as "big and as bad" as they want to be, in total anonymity of course. Nonetheless, I laughed at their cowardly tactics and continued on with my message of empowering Cincinnatians through education and dignity. Although I didn't get elected, I earned 7,499 votes in my first attempt at political office. With my integrity in tact, I vowed to run as Andre Harper, and to win or lose as Andre Harper.

Despite the Democratic Party's legacy of murder and intimidation with no evidence of ever improving our situation, it wields enormous power over African-Americans. The most powerful way and the inspiration of this book, is the enslavement of the African American mind. The plantation is no longer a physical place, it is not bound geographically, it's much worse. They have placed a concrete wall around the minds of the African-American community in order to control their actions and votes. A wall that is fortified with misinformation, intimidation, guilt trips for those who consider alternatives and threats should you select one. These walls can't be broken without tremendous sacrifice. Much like the slaves of old that were controlled by fear of physical beatings, today's political plantation is controlled by the fear of rejection and having to depend on their own ability.

It just seems natural for Democrats to use intimidation instead of engaging in the intellectual arena. In 2009, with a veto proof majority in the Senate, super-majority in the House and a liberal Democrat president, the Democrats can do anything they want. Healthcare reform was one of their goals. There is nothing the GOP can do to stop them except voice opposition. Yet the Democrats, who used to advocate freedom of speech, are not only threatening the GOP to back away from opposing reform, they are now threatening the American electorate. I don't think George Orwell could even comprehend what we are living through.

Whether people agree or disagree with President Obama, freedom to address your elected representatives used to be protected by the Constitution. Perhaps taking away basic constitutional rights is what he meant by calling the Constitution a "charter of negative liberties" meaning that it doesn't say "what the states can't do to you, [it] says what the federal government can't do to you, but it doesn't say what the federal government or the state government must do on your behalf."[38] Even though they have complete control they still need to make those who oppose their desires into villains.

The Obama White House vowed to squash any Americans that had the nerve to voice opposition to health care at their congressional town hall discussions by unleashing thousands of organizers to intimidate dissenters. I got an email from Obama asking me to intimidate others into forfeiting their constitutional right to voice opposition. It read, "This is the moment our movement was built for," to get me hyped up. Then he obviously thought that I was an uniformed lemming who couldn't think for himself so he started with the emotion stirring misinformation by saying, "There are those who profit from the status quo, or see this debate as a political game, and they will stop at nothing to block reform. They are filling the airwaves and the internet with outrageous falsehoods to scare people into opposing change. And some people, not surprisingly, are getting pretty nervous. So we've got to get out there, fight lies with truth, and set the record straight." In order to get me to me to do his bidding he ran a guilt trip on me by saying "So yes, fixing this crisis will not be easy. Our opponents will attack us every day for daring to try. It will require time, and hard work, and there will be days when we don't know if we have anything more to give. But there comes a moment when we all have to choose between doing what's easy, and doing what's right. Can you commit to join at least one event in your community this month?" [39]

In a meeting to prepare Democrat senators for the dissenters and assure them that he had their backs, Jim Messina, the deputy White House chief of staff, said any advertising attack would be met with a bigger response from Obama and that "If you get hit, we will punch back twice as hard." [40] Obama did something that would really scare Orwell. From the official White House website, Linda Douglass, the communications director for the White House's Health Reform Office, encouraged Americans to send Obama information about people that they think are spreading information that Obama doesn't agree with. It said "There is a lot of disinformation about health insurance reform out there, spanning from control of personal finances to end of life care. These rumors often travel just below the surface via chain emails or through casual conversation. Since we can't keep track of all of them here at the White House, we're asking for your help. If you get an email or see something on the web about health insurance reform that seems fishy, send it to flag@whitehouse.gov."[41] Only God knows what they are going to do to those people whose information they collect. I suppose his chief of staff Rahm Emanuel will send them a dead fish like he did to the pollster that angered him.[42]

Democrats have convinced black people that our history started in the civil rights movement. They know that their entire political plantation will be jeopardized if blacks were to learn the Democrat's true role in the "Black Holocaust." Therefore it is in their best interest to suppress the African-American awareness of their history and culture. The liberal "Black Holocaust" deniers know that their stranglehold on our votes is directly tied to their ability to keep us in political bondage.

All of their rhetoric and propaganda is designed to make us believe that the last 40 years of them "fighting" for our civil rights is much more important than the previous 400 years in which at least half of that the Democratic Party was directly responsible for perpetuation of the "Black Holocaust" in which thousands upon thousands of black people were slaughtered. They don't like to talk about how their policies have destroyed thousands of black families, leaving many of us unable to trace our lineage. They have led us to believe that token gestures of kindness make up for the destruction they continue to cause.

How Do You Hold Liberals Accountable?

I also found it troubling that I could not find any consistent principles that their party stands for. Their guiding principles consist of their 50 state political strategy, the platform (which changes every convention), charters and bylaws, and their political agenda. They have no moral standards. Perhaps that's why high-profile marital infidelity and corruption is not met with much public outrage (or perhaps the media just refuses to cover it), while the GOP is scrutinized heavily because they do claim to have a moral compass. The Republican principles transcend time and issues. We all understand that conditions change but principles and beliefs should be a guiding light when difficult times arise. This is distinguished from the Democrats, who change their party beliefs every four years in order to keep up with the shifting political winds. I found it great that the Democratic Party strives for things like honest leadership, an open government, national security, energy independence, economic prosperity, educational excellence, a healthcare system that works for everyone, and retirement security. I don't think they'd find too many people who are against those things. However, they do make pathetic attempts to convince the electorate that Republicans aren't for these things. It's a good thing people aren't as dumb as the DNC would have us be.

I also found it humorous that on their website they boast that "the Democratic Party has a long and proud history of representing and protecting the interests of working Americans and guaranteeing personal liberties for all." When did this start? They take credit for being the oldest party in operation in this country which dates back to 1792, but by all accounts black people couldn't vote until February 3, 1870 and women couldn't vote until August 18, 1920! The worst part about this lie is that the Democratic Party fought vigorously against both these measures. They also mentioned that they are proud of their history which tells me that they feel no shame about their well-

102

documented racist and sexist past. [43] I am sure they are proud of all of the Native Americans that Andrew Jackson slaughtered during his Indian Removal from the South.

Their use of masking themselves as the party of the people has cleverly disguised their usage of class warfare to divide the nation in their quest for political domination. As we learned with New York Democratic Governor Elliot Spitzer, the best way to cover up your misdeeds is to vigorously blame someone else for doing the same things you are doing. He relentlessly went after enemies who were allegedly involved in prostitution and other crimes while he was heavily engaged in the same activity. [44] We also learned that what goes on in the dark will one day come to light. This book is designed to shine a light on the Democrats consistent use of dividing our nation for political gain.

I concluded that the Democrats are more concerned with acquiring and maintaining political power than making our country better. I believe that their loyalty is not with the American people, but with of the desires of the party. When I studied the history of their party, I found that this is consistent with why they highly regard pioneer Andrew Jackson. They employ the same ruthless tactics he used when he controlled their party. I am sure that President Jackson is very proud of his party right now.

Shutting Up the Opposition

I am an avid listener of talk radio. I tune into both the conservative and urban talk shows, listening for the differing and most often conflicting positions on various issues. I enjoy contrasting the various advertisements. Rarely will I hear the same ads. The tone and language spoken by the advertisers are always distinctly different. The thing I love the most about listening to the various stations and hosts is that I get to hear so many differing points of view so that I can make the most informed decisions. The stations that contain these shows can schedule programming based on their demographics in order to maximize their listening audience and profits because they know the radio industry much better than bureaucrats in Washington DC. The only problem is that conservative talk radio has grown in amount of listeners, profits, and most importantly voter influence since the fairness doctrine was defeated in the late 1980's when the Supreme Court declared it an unconstitutional contradiction of the Constitution as well as bad policy.[45]

The Fairness Doctrine was started by the FCC in 1949 to regulate the airwaves. The rule eventually became to "afford reasonable opportunity for discussion of contrasting points of view on controversial matters of public importance." Of course the fairness doctrine was intended to be anything but "fair." It was designed by elite political operatives to suppress political opposition in the budding radio era. Bill Ruder, Democratic campaign strategist and Assistant Secretary of Commerce in the Kennedy Administration said it best when he said "Our massive strategy was to use the Fairness Doctrine to challenge and harass right-wing broadcasters and hope the challenges would be so costly to them that they would be inhibited and decide it was too expensive to continue."[46] Throughout their history the Democratic Party has used shaping (and breaking) the law to intimidate political opponents in their quest for absolute power as standard operating procedures. The fairness doctrine is a part of the evolution that includes slave codes, the Ku Klux Klan, and Jim Crow laws. The Democrats want to use the Fairness Doctrine as 21st century method of burning crosses in an opponent's lawn. To no surprise Nancy Pelosi and her henchmen want to bring back the Fairness Doctrine at all costs and she won't let an insignificant thing like the Constitution get in the way for her quest for absolute power.

In 2007, House Speaker Nancy Pelosi stated that the federal government would mandate "fairness" in broadcasting. She reportedly said that House leaders would "aggressively pursue" legislation to reinstate the "Fairness Doctrine." [47] Just like many other disingenuous liberal politicians she wants to masquerade her assault on free speech and conservative talk radio by calling for fairness. Her goal is to silence her critics.

She only wants to apply this level of regulation on talk radio and not other forms of communication like television, cable, newsprint, and the internet. The truth is that conservatives don't have a monopoly on talk radio. Liberals are free to start their own radio shows. In fact, they have. The problem is that no one listens and they are not profitable. Imagine that. I live in Cincinnati and I remember advertising for Jerry Springer's (Cincinnati's Former mayor) liberal radio show being shoved down our throats for weeks. The show was taken off of the air in a matter of weeks because no one listened.

Talk show hosts like Rush Limbaugh, Sean Hannity and Glenn Beck have made fortunes spreading the good news of conservatism on their radio programs. Liberals accuse people who don't agree with them, especially conservative talk radio hosts of spewing "hate speech" when they are simply exercising their Constitutional right of free speech. Most importantly they refuse to abide by the ever moving liberal standards of political correctness. Liberals are always threatened by opposing ideologies and free thinkers. Limbaugh in particular has become public enemy #1 by the liberal elite. He was one of the pioneers of conservative radio after the tyranny of the Fairness Doctrine was abolished in the 1980's because they were able to express their opinions without fear of being punished by regulators. Their free speech was no longer exclusive to the political elite. Although he is a private citizen and not an elected official, the liberals relentlessly go after him because he exercises the same constitutional right in which they hold dear. Can you say hypocrisy?

In a futile attempt to bully Rush, Senate Majority Leader Harry Reid tried (and I use that loosely) to threaten Rush's livelihood by calling on Mark P. Mays, president of Clear Channel Communications, to denounce remarks made Limbaugh when he referred to U.S. troops opposing the war in Iraq as "phony soldiers" in response to (the liberal puppeteers) MoveOn.org ad that referred to Gen. David Petraeus as "General Betray Us." As part of the smear campaign, Reid got 41 Democrat senators to sign a letter condemning Rush's use of free speech. Rush auctioned the letter and raised over $45,000 where one hundred percent of the proceeds went to educate the children of Marines and law enforcement officers who died while on duty. [48] If you listen to Limbaugh, you would know that there isn't a more vocal supporter in word and deeds of our servicemen. Unlike Reid, his integrity won't allow him to use their sacrifice in political game of one-upmanship.

Limbaugh is also a target of Democratic Party boss Howard Dean who frequently uses his position to attack Rush's constitutional rights. He lampooned Rush's abuse of painkillers on Meet the Press. He even did an impression of Limbaugh snorting cocaine in front of a Democrat gathering in Minnesota.

He is the standard bearer of the liberal party that believes in equality, fairness and protecting people's feelings. When questioned about the appropriateness of his statements, he defended his actions by saying that "Democrats have strong moral values. Frankly, my moral values are offended by some of the things I hear on programs like 'Rush Limbaugh,' and we don't have to put up with that." [49] This is further proof that liberals are terrorized by the thought that others don't bow to their feet or leave their positions unchallenged.

Within the first week of Obama's election he made it a point to find a new conservative to become the physical representation of the enemy of the Democrats since George W. Bush was gone. Although they continue to blame Bush, even they are bright enough to know that wouldn't last forever, therefore it was imperative to find another target. That person became Rush Limbaugh. The president and the Democrats attack Limbaugh for one reason --- they don't like what he stands for because he has no real power. As a radio host, he can't enact legislation, he can't grant any government appointments, he can't make any executive orders, and he has no influence over tax policies. His only crime is using his constitutionally protected freedom of speech.

When President Obama tried to push his trillion dollar pork plan, also called the stimulus, he told Republicans not to listen to Limbaugh if they wanted to get along with Democrats and the new administration. He said "You can't just listen to Rush Limbaugh and get things done." Obama wants people to know that disagreement will not be accepted. He wants all to know that opposition is considered treasonous and for those Republicans like Rep. Eric Cantor (R-Va.), that forgot who won the elections, he reminded them. Our arrogant leader stated "I won" and "I will trump you on that." [50] I suppose that's how our benevolent leader gains consensus.

The Democrats took their marching orders and moved further. After the liberal media purposely distorted Limbaugh's recent comment stating that he hopes President Obama "fails," the Democratic Congressional Campaign Committee launched a petition drive ultimately designed to remove the conservative radio host from the airwaves. [51] The Democrat's are trying to get rid of any voices of opposition. On their website they wrote "Stand strong against Rush Limbaugh's Attacks — sign our petition, telling Rush what you think of his attacks on President Obama." They are basically telling people that THEY will decide the difference between critics and attacks. This means that when they are the opposition, their comments are criticism. When they are in control, then others opposition are attacks. This is a blatant attempt to close ranks around their president.

The same hypocrites must have forgotten the previous eight years and all of their vitriol towards Pres. George Bush. I think Hillary Clinton said it best when she said "I'm sick and tired of people who say that if you debate and disagree with this administration, somehow you're not patriotic. We need to stand up and say we're Americans, and we have the right to debate and disagree with any administration." [52] In typical Democratic fashion it is always a diabolical plan behind their earnestly presented product because after those who oppose others' freedom of speech leave their comments, their information will be collected for fundraising purposes. [53]

During the 2008 Election, Sam Joe Wurzelbacher suddenly became known as Joe the Plumber because he wasn't enchanted by the anointed one Barack Obama. While Limbaugh is already wealthy, he is able to withstand the daily personal assualts from liberals while he challenges them in the arena of ideas. Joe learned that common people are also subject to these attacks on their families and livelihood. While Obama was campaining on Joe's property, he had the gall to ask Obama some serious questions about his tax policy because he was an aspiring business owner. Obama did his best to convice him not to be successful and depend on liberal's to provide for him by saying that he wanted to "spread the wealth around." This is the liberals way to steal from those that have earned and give to those that have not. Obama only revealed what all liberals believe but are too cowardly to say aloud. As a result of his insubordination, Joe was subject to intimidation, humiliation and investigations by cowardly liberals, the Democratic Party and the media. Obama mocked him at a rally[54] along with Joe Biden[55]. ABC news ran a story about Joe's delinquent taxes and liberal blogs posted his home and work address. We all should learn that liberals should never be questioned and that you are only allowed to ask questions that make them favorable.

After the election, it was discovered that Democrat operatives inside of the Ohio Department of Job and Family Services were responsible for using state resources to find information about Joe in order to destroy him for asking the messiah a question. Gov. Ted Strickland suspended department director Helen Jones-Kelley, in addition to four more senior staffers, when they discovered Jones-Kelley improperly authorized searches of state databases to get information on Joe. She also improperly used her state e-mail account to raise money for Barack Obama. Ohio Inspector General Tom Charles reported that Jones-Kelley authorized searches on child support, unemployment compensation and public assistance.[56] People should think twice before they criticize President Obama, or any Democrat for that matter, because you could also be subject to personal attacks like the one Joe suffered. The safety of you and your family could be compromised because leading Democrats will put your personal information on the front page of the newspaper.

I refuse to be a pawn in Nancy Pelosi's and the liberal elite's quest for total control of the country. I don't owe them anything and my pride will never allow me to blindly follow a party that has continuously perpetrated the Black Holocaust. The legislative branch, specifically the House, was designed to be the representative voice of the people by carving the entire United States into 435 geographical districts. I can distinctly recall Democrats baselessly accusing the GOP of abuse of power while they were in the minority during the late 1990's and 2000's. During the GOP majority they would have never denied the Democrats an opportunity to speak as the Democrats have done.

During the Congressional recess of 2008, Pelosi and the Democrats took a page out of the shrewdest communist dictators by adjourning the House, turning off the lights, and killing the microphones, leaving the Republicans still on the floor. The GOP leadership refused to go on recess without addressing the high gas prices. The Democrats' friends at C-SPAN refused to broadcast the event so that American citizens couldn't witness the Democrat bullying. [57] Pelosi, in her infinite wisdom, decided that the minority party would not have their voices heard. She refused to debate the issue because she didn't feel that it was worthy of debate.

I don't usually take my political disagreements with liberals personally but I must make an exception for Nancy Pelosi. I don't know this woman personally, but I don't see much from her that gives me any confidence that I'd ever want to breathe the same air as her. I will personally never make any threats to her, like weak minded people do to people they don't like, because honestly harming a liberal is not worth one second of incarceration. Nonetheless, hypocrisy is a tenet of liberalism, and Nancy Pelosi is perhaps the biggest culprit.

5

RE-WRITING BLACK HISTORY

"History is a clock that people use to tell their time of day. It is a compass they used to find themselves on the map of human geography. It tells them where they are, and what they are."

—John Henrik Clarke

Often I hear black people say "well the Republicans may have done a lot for black people in the past, but they haven't done anything for us lately." When anyone makes this assumption, liberals celebrate because it means that they posses limited reasoning ability and therefore will be easily controlled. This person will accept anything liberals say as fact and all of their commands will be followed. It is a mistake for anyone to look at anything mankind does in isolation, especially politics. Anyone who thinks that people do things in isolation should remember Ephesians 6:12 which states "For we wrestle not against flesh and blood, but against principalities, against powers, against the rulers of the darkness of this world, against spiritual wickedness in high places." Despite the changing of the characters, the plan and desires of liberalism in America has remained constant. Anyone who fails to understand how incidents connect together is bound to be controlled by these evil forces in high places.

For anyone who believes that when the government provides welfare, public housing, and other self-determination destroying "services" the government is actually doing them a favor, they have clearly traded their pride for a few government freebies. Those assisted people fail to see that these government officials provide "benefits" by robbing the producers in society, which allows liberals to build a loyal voting base. This loyal base empowers Democrats to get and remain elected which allows them to accomplish their real goals (which aren't helping the poor.) Too often their voters are oblivious to everyday legislation which directly affects the rest of society. I am sure that having so many uniformed voters is perfectly fine with liberals. For liberalism to be truly effective, the overwhelming majority of their followers need to obey orders instead of question them. The real goal of any leftist movement is total control of everything. Their tactics evolve but their goal is constant, and those who don't learn this will be victims of it. Liberals also control black people by encouraging us to blindly trust them. This trust is dependent on blacks accepting that we are indeed unable to function and compete like other races due societal pressures. This notion is contrary our great past as well as what I have learned and believe.

One of the Many Benefits of an HBCU Education

One of the great aspects of attending a historically black college or university (HBCU) like Florida A&M University (FAMU), is that you are taught to learn about your history. Before I enrolled at FAMU, I had already been exposed to various parts of black history, but I had never truly studied it. Every student at FAMU is required to take a least one semester of African-American history. This may be enough exposure for most students but I wanted more so I minored in history. I learned early and often that the Democratic Party in America was, and is responsible for some of the greatest atrocities ever committed against the black man. I learned that the party sanctioned disenfranchisement and murder in order to advance the Democrat agenda.[58] Black people in America need to either acknowledge the Democrats' role in the Black Holocaust and hold them accountable for it or stop mentioning racism and slavery as the causes of our condition in this country. You cannot have an honest discussion about slavery and racism without mentioning the names of those who are directly responsible for it, and those people are the Democratic Party. The fact that Black Democratic leaders refuse to mention the history of their party is proof positive of the slave mentality that exists among black people in today's Democratic Party.

I took American history classes, African-American history, and world history because it all ties together. One must look at the history of man to see how society has evolved. You will also find that situations may change but the nature of man doesn't. Throughout history, regardless of cultures, there has always been a social class establishment. In America we like to think that color is the basis of the differences in class. You will find that even in monochromatic societies, people find reasons to differentiate themselves from one another and thus determine which aspects make one group feel elevated above another.

For instance, in ancient West Africa (1300-1500) there were class structures in place even in the absence of the state long before the Europeans arrived. Most people lived in communities where the hierarchy was dictated by monarchs who claimed divine or semi-divine status. Although many didn't have absolute power, they did control the armies, taxed commerce and accumulated considerable wealth when compared to that of the rank-in-file citizen. Beneath the royalty were classes of landed nobles, warriors, peasants, and bureaucrats. Lower classes included blacksmiths, butchers, weavers, woodcarvers, tanners and the oral historians called griots. Since ancient times, slavery had always been a part of the hierarchal society structure in West Africa while it was less prominent in other places. Like in other places in the world, slaves - men, women and children - were generally prisoners of war. The length of servitude and living conditions varied. [59]

In more primitive civilizations where "might is right" the strongest leaders were able to take over using intimidation and force, or were the ones who convinced others that they descended from divine lineage. We've seen this in many cultures where dictators coordinate violent coups to oust the sitting leadership. Generally the leader becomes too strong and rules his countrymen with an iron fist. Eventually a courageous outsider takes over who promises to be different than his predecessor. There is an old saying "power tends to corrupt; absolute power corrupts absolutely." Without checks and balances the courageous new leader eventually becomes the very person that he removed.

The founders of the United States must have known this. I believe this is why they set up our government structure the way that it is in order to prevent such acts. The founders established three branches of government in order to have checks and balances. Whereas other societies depend on brute strength to seize control of the government, our society depends more on the manipulation of intelligence and emotion in order to seize power at the ballot box. The Democratic Party in the United States has taught us that one of the best ways to seize power and solidify a voting base is to rewrite history and then repeatedly

119

tell your followers what you want them to believe enough times until they believe it. You have to also make them feel so comfortable that they have no desire to challenge your assertions or be compelled to do their own homework. This is the case of Democrat's approach to the African-American community.

The Real History of the Democratic Party

For several generations now, my people have loyally given their votes to the Democratic Party and have suffered because of it. The Democrats have shoved the idea down our throats that they are our best hope for success, and that the Republicans are evil people who hate us because we are black. The Democratic mantra and ever-changing philosophies have had a devastating effect on our families, our economy, our dignity, the quality of education we receive, and our ambition. I've heard on more than one occasion the phrase "if you don't know where you've come from, then you won't know where you're going." I took that to heart. In fact, the first thing I did when I decided to sever my ties to the Democratic Party was to do a history lesson for myself. I decided to see how much truth there was to what I had been told all of my life. Not only did I find out that the Democratic Party was lying about their service to contemporary African-Americans, they have been lying about their role in the entire African-American experience.

The notion that the Democratic Party has ever been concerned about the well-being of African-Americans is a complete lie. The Democrats' own history tells you that they were not only "the white man's party" in the past, it remains the same today. Sure they have "diversity" in the tent but the organizational leaders remain white men including Gov. Howard Dean, Democratic National Committee Chairman; West Virginia Gov. Joe Manchin, Democratic Governors Association Chairman; Sen. Charles Schumer (D-NY), Democratic Senatorial Campaign Committee Chairman; Rep. Chris Van Hollen (D-MD), Democratic Congressional Campaign Committee Chairman; and Iowa Senate Majority Leader Mike Gronstal, Democratic Legislative Campaign Committee Chairman.[60] As the oldest remaining political party in the world, the Democratic Party continues to unleash its wrath on black people. Each generation the tactics have changed with the mission remaining the same. Howard Dean, is an extension of his forefathers. He maintains the original mission of the Democratic Party which is to keep the white man at the top of the pecking order in America.

Sure you can say that both parties have white male leadership at the top. The difference is that one talks about the importance of people's colors while the other talks about the importance of people's content. The Democrats are quick to accuse others of racism and stand behind the threats of legal action in order to force entities to colorize. When you look at the top of their party leadership, you can't tell if it is 1829 or 2009.

The Democratic Party was formed in 1792, when supporters of Thomas Jefferson began using the name Democrat Republicans, or Jeffersonian Republicans, to emphasize its anti-aristocratic policies. In 1789 it adopted the moniker of the "party of the common man." I believe this is where they began encouraging followers to believe that they are no longer individually special but are "common" like everyone else, and that excellence was reserved for people like Jackson who convinced them that he was somehow bestowed with knowledge and abilities that they could never acquire. This set the stage for instilling the belief that success is reserved for the few and the "common" people should have faith but most importantly, trust in the leaders.

It dropped the Republican name during the Presidency of Andrew Jackson in the 1830s.[61] Southern Democrats insisted on protecting slavery in all the territories while many Northern Democrats resisted. The Democratic Party identified itself as the "white man's party" and demonized the Republican Party for welcoming black people into their ranks. [62] Despite being defeated in the Civil War the Democratic Party was determined to re-capture the South by any means necessary. They gained power through the ballot, through intimidation, discrimination, and the murder of countless African Americans. By 1877, when Reconstruction was officially over, the Democratic Party dominated the South for a century until the Civil Rights movement began in the 1960s. [63]

The Democratic Party was determined to maintain white supremacy and black inferiority for the preservation of the institution of slavery. The Republican Party was founded primarily to counter this notion. The Republican Party was officially formed in July 1854 in Jackson, Michigan. The platform adopted at the party's first national convention in 1856 totally rejected slavery. In 1860, Abraham Lincoln became the first Republican president who selected pro-civil war Tennessee Democrat Andrew Johnson as his vice president. After Lincoln's assassination, Johnson became the president and inherited a Republican controlled Congress. The Democratic Johnson wanted to re-admit the Democrat-controlled Southern states back into the Union and allow them to individually define the status of blacks. However, the Republican-controlled Congress wanted the federal government to ensure black rights. [64]

Much to the dismay of the Democratic Party, the Republicans won the battle for control of Reconstruction and passed the 14th and 15th amendments to the Constitution, seeking to guarantee blacks the right to due process of law and the vote. The Republicans, America's true party of diversity,

123

established a bi-racial coalition. Black Republicans won hundreds of elected positions, from local government to Congress, and were appointed to many administrative positions. During Reconstruction, the Republican controlled Congress established the Bureau of Refugees, Freedmen, and Abandoned Lands (The Freedman's Bureau) which was created by Congress in March 1865 to assist for one year in the transition from slavery to freedom in the South. The Bureau was asked to help the Southern blacks and whites make the transition from slavery to freedom, by introducing a system of free labor, overseeing some 3,000 schools and enforcing labor contracts between blacks and whites. The Freedman's Bureau made way for the establishment of a number of colleges and training schools for blacks, including Howard University and Hampton Institute. Democrat President Andrew Johnson opposed having the federal government secure black rights and thought The Freedman's Bureau was unconstitutional. [65]

The resilient Democratic Party refused to accept a society where black people would be considered equal. Under the banner of white supremacy, Southern Democrats used violence, fraud, intimidation and murder to win elections. When Republicans lost interest in the South, President Rutherford B. Hayes formally ended Reconstruction in what was known as the Compromise of 1877, which left African-Americans at the mercy of Southern Democrats. Soon members of the Democratic

124

Party would form America's original domestic terrorism organization that would haunt African-Americans for years to come. [66]

The Ku Klux Klan was formed as a social club by a group of Confederate Army veterans in Pulaski, Tennessee in the winter of 1865-66. The Klan members dressed in robes and sheets, intended to prevent identification by the occupying federal troops (and to frighten blacks.) The Klan quickly became a terrorist organization in service of the Democratic Party and white supremacy. Between 1869 and 1871 its goal was to destroy Congressional Reconstruction by murdering blacks -- and some whites -- who were either active in Republican politics or educating black children.[67] Many state public officials throughout the nation were members. The Klan did the bidding of the Democratic Party by burning churches and schools which drove thousands of people out of their homes. In response to local law enforcement officials being unable or unwilling to stop the Klan, Congress passed the Force Bill in 1871, giving the federal government the power to prosecute the Klan. Despite these laws the Klan continued to burn crosses, torture and murder those they opposed through the Civil Rights era. [68]

As a result of the Democratic Party's willingness to use illegal tactics to win elections, they acquired seniority in Washington, DC which allowed them to control most of the committees in both houses of Congress and kill any civil rights legislation. The South remained a one-party region until the Civil Rights movement began in the 1960s. Northern Democrats, most of whom had prejudicial attitudes towards blacks, offered no challenge to the discriminatory policies of the Southern Democrats. With their power and seniority, the Southern Democrats were rarely challenged by liberal president Franklin Delano Roosevelt during the 1930s and '40s. Protecting the rights of black people is only a top priority for liberals in words and not in deed. He rarely challenged their power which allowed Southern senators to kill several federal anti-lynching bills in the 1930s by filibuster. In addition to intimidating presidents, the Southern Democrats also had control of the party's agenda. [69]

Liberals and the Civil Rights Movement

Northern Democrats, like the Kennedys, offered no challenge to the discriminatory policies of the Southern Democrats because ultimately they benefited from it. Even intelligent people like Barack Obama, that know better, would like for you to have a romantic view of Kennedy and Black America. However the reality is well documented that John F. Kennedy shared similar prejudicial attitudes towards blacks as his Southern party mates. Southern Democrats looked down on blacks because of their race while elitist Northern Democrats looked down on blacks because of their class. Despite how

126

Kennedy may have felt about blacks, he still needed them if he were to win the presidency. In fact, Kennedy campaigned saying that he would help improve civil rights only to get elected and did everything he could to avoid the topic once he won the White House. History teaches us that John F. Kennedy had no plans for making the civil rights movement an important part of his legacy. In fact, he didn't trust Martin Luther King and authorized FBI surveillance so the government would be aware of his activities.

During the 1960s, Dr. King was considered the "most dangerous ... effective Negro leader" in U.S. by J. Edgar Hoover and the Federal Bureau of Investigation.[70] In July 1963, nearly a month before the March on Washington, Democrat Attorney General Robert Kennedy consented to a plan that allowed the FBI to tap the phones of King and his associates in order to bug their homes and offices. They also were permitted to secretly track the movements of Dr. King and his associates. Kennedy gave the FBI permission to break into King's office and home to install the bugs, as long as agents recognized the "delicacy of this particular matter" and didn't get caught installing them. However, Kennedy would only agree to the surveillance if he was personally informed of any pertinent information. The surveillance allowed the government to discover embarrassing details about King's sex life, which the FBI used against him in the form of anonymous harassment and threats to go public in

127

order to embarrass him. None of this would have happened without the consent of the Kennedys. [71]

Democrats love to take credit for their role in passing civil rights legislation in the 1960's by touting it as the centerpiece of the Democratic Party's civil rights accomplishments. The Voting Rights Act of 1965 was nothing more than an illusion used to convince African-Americans that they had finally achieved equality. It gave the civil rights movement a tangible measure of success. First of all, you can not ignore the fact that there would not have been a need for the civil rights legislation had it not been for the Democratic Party's hundred years of violently disenfranchising blacks after the passage of the 13th, 14th and 15th amendments passed by Republicans. Had it not been for their illegal and terrorist activities against African-Americans there would not have been any need for this legislation. President Lyndon Johnson and the Democrats pulled the wool over the eyes of black America by signing ceremonial legislation into law on August 6, 1965 that was used to prohibit practices used by his own Democratic Party. Furthermore if black people take the time to read the civil rights legislation they will find that it is virtually redundant when compared to more definitive legislation. [72]

This episode of our history is very important because it helps President Johnson appear larger than life as a champion of black people, magnifying the perception of the power of the presidency. Despite the opposition from many in his party, since the president was a Democrat, his party received the credit for the passage of the legislation and history will ignore the work of Republican Sen. Everett Dirksen who played a big role in its passage as well. The passage of the Voting Rights Act of 1965 made it easy for the Democrats (with continued reiteration from their black appointed black leaders) to fool black people into believing that all power flows from the government and that the president is king. White people know that it doesn't matter who holds the office because they will protect and defend their constitutional rights. Democrats use their resources to convince black people into believing that without a Democrat president and Democrats in elected office to support him, black people are left unprotected. Democrats have a vested interest in making sure that black people continue to accept this premise without dispute. By insisting that black people learn how the government works, how the three branches work together, and individual rights provided by the Constitution, it will surely pose a challenge in maintaining control of blacks on their political plantation.

Legalized Terror

I suppose there was a need for the Voting Rights Act because it was common practice during those times for the Democratic Party to use their enforcers in the Klan to murder and intimidate black people in order to maintain political power in the South. From Reconstruction until now, the most powerful elected Democrats used their elected positions to maintain White supremacy. I learned from the "Tom Joyner Morning Show" that powerful Democrats like former governor and Senator of Georgia, Herman E. Talmadge, adamantly opposed Civil Rights Legislation and school integration. Talmadge denounced the 1954 Supreme Court decision on school desegregation by saying "there aren't enough troops in the whole United States to make the white people of this state send their children to school with colored children." [73]

Another Democratic legend who was determined to maintain white superiority through politics was former governor of Alabama, George Wallace. The four-time governor of Alabama and four-time candidate for president of the United States was known as the embodiment of resistance to the civil rights movement. Wallace was elected governor the first time in 1962, with what was the largest popular vote in state history. In his Inaugural address he declared: "I draw the line in the dust and toss the gauntlet before the feet of tyranny, and I say, segregation now, segregation tomorrow, segregation forever." Wallace became a national figure in 1963 when he kept a campaign promise to stand "in the schoolhouse door" to block integration of Alabama public schools. [74] On June 11, 1963, he and armed state troopers barred the path of two black students attempting to

130

register at the University of Alabama defying federal orders. While campaigning in Maryland's Democratic presidential primary in 1972, he was shot, which left him paralyzed from the waist down.

Like Alabama, the state of Mississippi was also a civil rights battleground where the Democratic Party used the government as a tool to suppress and murder black people. On Monday, May 17, 1954, the United States Supreme Court unanimously outlawed racial segregation in public schools in *Brown v. Board of Education*. In the south, this day became known as "Black Monday" and served as a rallying call in order to preserve segregation as their way of life. The Democratic Party in the south rejected the nation's changing views on racial equality and was determined to combat the mounting civil rights movement in the South. Lifelong Democrat and Mississippi Governor James Coleman and the Democrat controlled legislature created the Mississippi State Sovereignty Commission to counter attacks on racism in the Deep South.

The Mississippi State Sovereignty Commission was a taxpayer-funded terrorist organization, sanctioned by the Democratic Party of Mississippi. The Commission was tasked to maintain the state's segregation and cherished "southern way of life" through legal and illegal means. The Commission hired agents who were empowered to tap phones, gather information on, as well as interrogate suspected civil rights activists. [75] This government agency used this information to contact local media who would print this information, send letters to subjects' employers, and even gave private information to Ku Klux Klan who acted as the agencies enforcers. The Klan would use the information to terrorize, intimidate, and eliminate anyone who stood in the way of the goals of the commission. The commission acted in this matter throughout the civil rights movement until it was finally dissolved in 1973.[76] However, history should not forget the thousands of innocent people that this Democrat sanctioned terrorist commission disenfranchised and murdered.

There are countless stories where the Democrats hid behind the law in order to infringe upon the rights of African-Americans throughout the history of the United States. Despite the Democrats' state sponsored apartheid, and the other policies that have destroyed our communities, African-Americans still continue to blindly and loyally support the Democrat power grasp. When black people like me present the facts about crimes the Democratic Party has committed against my people, I am usually met with rejection, denial, closed minds and often hostility. I don't necessarily fault my people for this, because they have been trained by their Democratic masters not to think objectively, individually or to learn the history of the Democratic Party much less their own. They are encouraged to insulate their minds from outside influences for fear of reprisal. Our refusal to acknowledge the Democratic Party as a political plantation manipulating the minds of African-Americans in order to maintain political power will result in the continued destruction of the black community and the country.

6

DON'T LET THE LIBERALS FOOL YOU: AMERICAN POVERTY ISN'T THE SAME

"Let not him who is houseless pull down the house of another, but let him work diligently and build one for himself, thus by example assuring that his own shall be safe from violence when built."

—Abraham Lincoln

I'm not the most driven man in the world. However, I do believe in the value of hard work. I do believe that in the United States if you are willing to work, then there will be an opportunity for you to succeed. Black people must not fall for the bait used by our leadership which convinces us that we are still living in the 1950's. I have learned that liberals have trained us to constantly focus on what others have instead of taking the necessary steps to get our own. This is why they want you to focus on disparities instead of empowerment. This form of manipulation continues to keep African-Americans as the permanent under-class that they brought us here to be. Whenever Negro leaders start talking about disparities, look out. This is a form of player hating sanctioned by their liberal masters and media accomplices that profit from black lethargy. My life has convinced me that liberals expect me to be nothing so that they can be there to save me.

I will be the first to admit that 50 years ago, black people didn't have the opportunities that we have today and that alleged "glass ceiling" was much closer to my grandfather's head than it is to mine. I know that a lot of these so-called civil rights leaders want people to believe that we haven't made any progress over the last 300 years, but if you just look at their individual bank accounts and quality of life, you'll know better. Look no further than Jeremiah Wright who had a $1.6 million palace built in the whitest part of Chicago courtesy of the tithes and offerings of his Southside congregation, many of who I am sure he would never allow to walk inside. [77]

Liberals believe that only the ones they choose should be able to prosper in this country. They want you to be convinced that socio-economics and racism prevent black people from prospering in this country and only a few elitists like Henry Gates and Michael Eric Dyson have enough intestinal fortitude to escape poverty, conquer the system and "make it." Once they "make it" they seem to think that the best way to help the rest of us is to arm us with enough intelligent sounding excuses while we remain behind. Obama explained it when he got a few laughs at the expense of Joe the Plumber. "That a plumber is the guy he's fighting for..." Obama said to laughter at a rally. "How many plumbers you know making a quarter million dollars a year?"[78] The guy never said he made that much. He aspired to make that one day. Obama and his cronies expect people outside of the liberal graces to remain ignorant and dependent in order to fulfill their bloated egos and desire to feel relevant. It really disgusts me to know that the Democratic Party does not desire to empower people in their party, or anyone else for that matter. Just look around. They constantly push programs that keep people in programs. If I were to become a recipient of a low income program, the goal would be for me to one day rise out of the low income bracket, so that I could sustain myself and my family. I believe that a man should work. A man should earn what he needs for his family so that they will be proud to call him father and husband. The left wing of American society has removed the pride in a man taking care of his family. They have made it acceptable for a man to decide whether or not he wants to honor his responsibilities. Any male can make a baby, but it takes a man to ~~take~~ raise one. Not only have the Democrats given men the option of being responsible, they have enabled women to become single mothers and encourage more children out of wedlock through easily accessible state provided benefits. In essence they encourage poverty by accepting and encouraging irresponsibility.

The goal of the government should be to create self-sufficient people that increase tax revenue. These citizens should believe that it is their responsibility to be reliant upon their own God-given talents in order to contribute to a functioning society where everyone plays a role in the success. I believe that this is man's natural instinct. Instead, the Democrats benefit from people who believe that it is perfectly natural for someone else to provide their needs. I don't believe that they even consider this behavior as consumption of other's resources. Where the resources come from is of no concern to people with this thought process. However when the resources are discontinued or interrupted, it will result in protests and unruly behavior. The Democrats seem to forget that their state sponsored charity only works when other people are robbed of their earnings. I wonder what would happen if every working American quit working and became dependent on the government to provide benefits. The country would collapse immediately.

Declaration of War on the Black Family

Furthermore, it is infuriating to hear about Democrat's "war on poverty." First of all, God, the almighty one himself, says in the Bible that poverty will always be among us. In my opinion, trying to get rid of something that God told us would always be here directly challenges his word. Then again, no one ever accused them of believing in God in the first place. Nonetheless, since Lyndon Johnson's presidency, this country has poured billions of dollars into the war against poverty, resulting in more entitlement spending, more poverty, worse education, deteriorating inner cities, escalating crime rates and white flight - I think you get the picture. This sustained effort in destroying the will of black Americans has also resulted in seemingly permanent Democrat electoral majorities in these places as well. America itself has worsened since enacting socialist legislation like the "New Deal" and the "Great Society." At the same time the Democrats have solidified key voting blocs, which was probably their goal to begin with. The truth is that the government, white people, society, or anyone else can address poverty but only the person in poverty has the power to overcome it through education, hard work and good choices. There are no shortcuts. There is no magic. It will take time and commitment.

Of course the Democratic Party doesn't want you to understand that every time a person rejects welfare and decides to contribute their share to society, they stand to lose another voter, especially if they look at the effort that they are exerting and wonder why they are forced to carry the weight of other capable people. When people understand that each person has to pull their share, people realize the blessings of hard work. They understand that it is difficult to pull the weight of someone that has the same ability as you but chooses not to use it. This is when the GOP's message of self-worth, personal responsibility, and freedom to choose your lifestyle becomes appealing. More importantly, the Democrats often forcefully attempt to intimidate others into embracing their guilt ridden message tracks of paying higher taxes in order to subsidize others while your benefits are diminishing. One of my biggest issues with the Democratic Party is their lack of desire or commitment to personal development. They love to throw out phrases like "low income" and "the poor." Of course they follow that phrase with "who tend to be African American." As a proud black man I get angry every time I hear someone mention low income and African-American as being synonymous. When white people say it, I get upset; when black people say it, I get even angrier because many are selling out their own communities for a few program dollars.

Liberals know that with knowledge there's power; that's why it's critical that they control the flow of information. I, like so many other people, have learned that a quality education is the best way to combat poverty. I am a proud product of the Palm Beach County public school system and Florida A&M University, the world's greatest institution of higher learning, which happens to be a public institution. However, I understand that traditionally private schools have a reputation of providing a higher quality education than their public counterparts. As a parent, I want the best education for my children, which means that one day I may be forced to pay for private school tuition should the need arise because I know that a quality education is the only way that my children will be able to compete in a competitive global environment. Liberals understand this as well. This is why so many of the most prominent ones who claim to support the public school system are private school educated.

In words, racist liberals like Sen. Dick Durbin, who graduated from a private high school and private Georgetown University (BS & JD), claim to support the education of black children but his legally binding legislation says otherwise. Liberals can play semantics until eternity; it's the wording of the legislation you should be concerned with.

Many in the media have called the D.C. education program "controversial" because it gives about 1,700 low-income children scholarships worth up to $7,500, paid for with federal taxpayer dollars each year to cover costs of attending private schools rather than the traditionally low performing D.C. public schools.[79] Only racist liberals would call the program that provides great educations to black children "controversial." Ironically this voucher program, which has helped so many black children, was created in 2003 by a Republican-led Congress, and was vehemently opposed by the Democrats. However, this program is very popular among black residents who undyingly support these Democrats.

Republicans insist that parents deserve a choice if their kids are in failing schools, while Democrats, who are controlled by the teachers' unions, put their needs over the concerns of black children, and claim that public dollars are being siphoned away to private schools. If the goal is to provide a quality education then why does it matter if they kid is taught at a

141

private school since the government would have to pay for the child to attend school somewhere anyway? Other cities and states like Milwaukee, Cleveland, Florida, Utah, Arizona and Georgia have similar programs that are paid for with local tax dollars.[80] For Democrats, this is bigger than simply deciding where the funding goes, this is about keeping black children in failing environments so that they can continue to perpetuate and grow their voting base. They have proven that they would prefer to leave all black kids in failing environments instead of helping some of them escape them. With this great opportunity, some of these children will be in a position to one day come back and help the others who weren't as fortunate. However, by having these children grow up to be powerful thinkers and contributors to society, this proves once again educated black people are a threat to the Democratic Party.

When it came up for renewal in 2009, the Democrat-controlled Congress let it be known that they care little about the education of black children in Washington D.C. and care less about what the local black leadership thinks about their priorities. A majority of the members of the D.C. Council, led by fellow Democrats, sent a letter to Secretary of Education, Democrat Arne Duncan, expressing solid support for continuing the voucher program. It stated that "we strongly urge you to stand with us in supporting these children and continuing the District's Opportunity Scholarship Program," and that "we believe we simply cannot turn our backs on these families because doing so will deny their children the quality education they deserve." [81] Turn their backs is exactly what they did because when you effortlessly receive 90% of black votes you don't have to do anything they ask. President Obama, who knows the value of education because he has always attended private schools, sided with the unions instead of the black children, and didn't seem to care that two bright black kids, who attend the prestigious Sidwell Friends along with his two daughters, will also be affected.

This situation illustrates a perfect example of how so many black people get so consumed by Democrats and their rhetorical speeches, which are not legally binding, and choose to ignore language in legislation, which is legally binding. Earlier in the congressional session the racist Democrat Illinois Senator Dick Durbin fought vigorously and successfully to end the program by adding to a spending bill that phases out the program. Mr. Durbin's amendment reads that no federal money can be spent on the program beyond 2010 unless Congress reauthorizes it and the D.C. Council approves. Although the black people on the D.C. Council may support the vouchers, the national Democratic Party doesn't. Of course, it's run by wealthy white people and driven by their agenda. What the liberal controlled media labeled a "compromise," President Obama proposed allocating enough funding for all 1,716 students program to continue receiving grants until they graduate from high school but to not allow any new students to join the program.[82] Obama's decision results in a certain demise of the program and the destruction of the hopes of so many black families who hoped (to borrow his word) to use this program to create a brighter future through education. This is a victory for the unions and yet another defeat for black families at the hands of the Democrats. Obama and the Democrats will continue to operate this way because they know that black people continue to support them, vigorously defend them, ignore their own needs, and never consider an alternative.

It's saddening that so many black people fix their mouths to say so many untrue statements. It is true that there will always be obstacles that we all must climb, but there are ones that we have created like school dropouts, truancy and broken families. When so called leaders get in front of mixed company (white people) and speak as if the black community is a helpless group of needy people, they give a fierce slap in the face to our ancestors and those pioneers who succeeded in the worst of times. They disrespect the great sacrifices made by people like Malcolm X., Martin Luther King Jr., Harriet Tubman and others who sacrificed their lives so that we could have better opportunities than they had. They died fighting so that we would one day be able to compete for (not be given) the fruits of this world. They believed that black people could compete with any man if given the opportunity to prove his worth. Our contemporary leadership wants the world to think that black people need everything handed to us because we can't grasp concepts like hard work and fortitude as every other race appears to do. They are content with us being the permanent under-class because it pays the bills. I disagree with that assessment and have dedicated my life to rejecting it. Today millions of black people are now given opportunities that many of us aren't taking advantage of.

President Lyndon Johnson is famous for his "war on poverty". I couldn't agree more with his statement and how he used it. However, his declaration of war was on the black family. The primary objective for anything a politician does is to gain political power for himself and his party. So as the head of the Democratic Party, LBJ had to devise a plan to solidify votes among the black community because they didn't trust Democrats at that time. In order to gain their trust, they developed welfare which has resulted in legions of dedicated voters at a tremendous cost to my people. The welfare system was also designed to destroy the black family because it mandated that a man could not be a part of the household. The government stripped black men of their pride by having them hide under beds and closets during home inspections. Just like in slavery, it forced mothers to hide prized possessions in order maintain the appearance of living a substandard life. It rewarded women for having children out of wedlock and remaining unmarried by increasing the benefits per child. I assume at the time the goodhearted liberals felt that they were helping those unfortunate black people. Although they may prescribe the living conditions for the poor black people, I am sure that none of them would live their lives the way they mandate other people to live. However, I believe they were fully aware that what they were doing would devastate my people for generations because Barry Goldwater explained it when running against LBJ, but the liberals cast him as a racist because he knew welfare was poisonous.

Since the beginning of LBJ's big government "Great Society" programs and his "Robin Hood" liberal mentality of robbing from the "rich" and giving to the "poor," which is only a clever way to market the redistribution of wealth, the condition of the very people he allegedly set out to help has worsened. His all out assault on the dignity of black people has plagued the community in the decades since its implementation. His programs took away the negative stigmas attached to accepting government handouts and made it an acceptable way of life. Relying on our collective effort and independence from the government was a source of pride for black people. Democrats had to find another way to get around the pride within the black community. Liberals realized that in order to control our minds and break our innate survival instincts, they had to convince us that we could not survive without social programs and government assistance. They figured that manipulating our children would be the perfect vehicle.

Since black people had attached negative stigmas to receiving welfare, liberals had to convince us that the money received was to benefit the children. That was the inroad they needed. Over time the needs would eventually expand, requiring more "assistance" and increasing dependency. Government dependency is just like getting hooked on drugs. Once it becomes apart of your lifestyle, the void it fills becomes hard to replace with your own device. The longer you require the "assistance" the bigger the void becomes and in time, the will (and personal sacrifice) needed to fill that void on your own presents potentially insurmountable odds to a person already suffering a lack of confidence. Therefore the best way to avoid the drug of government dependency is to not experiment with it, despite the temporary hardship you may encounter.

Author James Bovard noted that when blacks were slow to get on the program, Congress mandated food stamps and hired 100,000 of their recruiters who went into inner cities to convince more people to enroll.[83] These people were tasked to advocate, organize sit-ins and further convince people that they needed this assistance instead of empowering them through vocational training and educational pursuit. Reports from the Department of Agriculture stated that food stamp workers would often overcome people's pride by telling parents, "this is for your children." Bureaucrats at the time acknowledged that they were being challenged by the people's will to survive without this government mandated "assistance." It went on to say that "... the problem is not with welfare recipients but with low income workers: It is this group which recoils when anything remotely resembling welfare is suggested... with careful explanations... coupled with intensive outreach efforts... resistance from the 'too prouds' bending. [84] This let me know that the will of the black man and woman to survive on his own was great. The Democrats knew that it would take a focused and sustained effort in order to break Black people's wills down in order to be manipulated; therefore (as usual) they had to use the power of the government to force others to submit to their will.

Perhaps the best depiction of a family living on welfare is in the 1974 20th Century Fox feature film <u>Claudine</u> starring Diahann Carroll, James Earl Jones, and directed by John Berry. It is noted for being one of the few mainstream films featuring a predominantly African-American cast that wasn't a "Blaxploitation" film. The film tells the story of Claudine Price (Diahann Carroll), a single Black Harlem mother, living on welfare with six children, who finds love with garbage collector Rupert Marshall, played by James Earl Jones.[85] The two fall in love and want to get married but fear they would not be able to support the children without welfare. The movie has great scenes that really show the viewer what it was like to be on welfare during those times. One scene shows an invasive welfare inspector who zealously accuses Claudine of having a male companion, which Claudine vehemently denies. Before the inspection Claudine and her children feverishly hide all of their best things in order to make an appearance of humility. I believe that this film really explores just how damaging welfare and addictive government reliance is on not only the psyche of the African-American, but or anyone who becomes dependent on someone else. Despite many challenges the black family was represented in a dignified manner, a far cry from what we see today in today's media.

The Results of Liberalism in the Black Community

One needs to look no further than the Maury Povich show to see the results of what 40 years of liberal "assistance" programs have done to the black family. Maury provides a graphic representation of what happens when you create a family structure absent of a caring father, a moral foundation, and dignity. His programming is dominated with shows about women who don't know who the fathers of their children are, infidelity, and girls that have no respect for authority. I suppose it makes for great ratings to see a woman drag several men (I have seen as many as 18) to a TV taping to find out if he is the father of her child, only to hear Maury say the words "you are

149

NOT the father" when the paternity test results are revealed. Too often, the subjects are black people. Of course, the liberals and their handpicked Negro leaders make no mention of this behavior in their requests for grant funding or their Capital Hill speeches. Their testimony won't include how liberal legislation removing fathers from homes has created generations of people that have no understanding of the family structure or the importance of a father and mother raising children together.

We are taught to believe that white people have both parents and that black mothers raise children on their own in a situation where you see the daddy sometimes if at all. Of course, liberals need to perpetuate this destruction of the black family because if enough blacks like me reject this warped thinking by embracing marriage and family values, they will then lose thousands of the free African-American votes they depend on to remain our overseers. In all fairness to Povich, who I believe is a good person, he is only providing a product that is obviously very profitable. As a practicing capitalist, I am not mad at him. Nonetheless, as a proud black man, it hurts me to see my people misrepresenting our proud heritage.

The liberal media and the talking heads would like for you to ignore the violence in the Black community that they have created. The liberal talking heads on cable would rather focus on global warming or avoiding the extinction of the spotted owl before they ever care about the violent neighborhoods that they created. They could care less about black men killing each other as long as the ones who survive get out and vote Democrat. By legislating that fathers be banished from homes, and offering increased payments to mothers for having more children out of wedlock and discouraging marriage, the liberals destroyed the black family unit so they could gain political power. This investment has paid big dividends as it created a dependent class of citizens who don't value education or family structure. Married parents raising children has become nearly a foreign concept in my community. This can be traced to welfare and not slavery as many of the sellouts would like for you to believe. Black families stood a better chance of staying together during slavery and Jim Crow than they do today in the urban settings created and controlled by Democrats.

Fathers were being kicked out of homes in order to make sure the mother could get enough government money to take care of the kids. The Democrats purposely removed the black father from his natural role as a provider and protector. Now his children see him in a different light. They no longer respect him and he no longer respects himself. Without self-respect what is he? However, he will find self-respect somewhere. He finds it in the street among others who share the same burden. Society discards him as worthless and has forced his family, but most importantly, his offspring to see him that way as well. The liberals of the day knew that only destruction would come from destroying the Black Family unit. The Democrats knew that their politically calculated attempt to help the children would usurp the father's role, thus destroying his role in the community, just as they did during slavery.

The liberal policies of welfare created a breakdown of the family which has had a devastating effect on black males in particular. The father loses respect because he is no longer the provider and protector; the government has commandeered that role. The son grows to resent him for his absence and no longer sees him as a role model then seeks another to fill the void. That role is too often filled by someone he considers strong, like a gang member, because his perception of manhood has already been tainted. Time in prison becomes a testament of strength, while a married family man who obeys the law is perceived as weak. The gang member sees himself in the child because he had a similar experience. Former gang member and probation officer with Montgomery County, Ohio, Johnny Vance, says that youngsters recruited into the gang life exhibit the "5 H's: Helpless — a lack of self-esteem; Hopeless — a feeling of no future; Hungry — a need for nurturing and attention; Homeless — no steady place to call home; and Hugless — no love and affection in their life."[86] These conditions were created in order to get votes for Democrats. Based on the high polling numbers in the black community, I am sure the liberal elite thinks that it was a great investment. The Democrat policy created conditions where the Black Holocaust would shift from whites killing blacks to blacks killing blacks. The rising black male death toll, the educational failures and high incarceration rates are acceptable to people like Bob Beckel, Jim Carvile and Donna Brazille just as long as the Democrats keep winning elections.

LBJ's programs transformed a once proud people into generations of dependents who expect and rely on the kindness of others to provide their basic needs, and have accepted living in the lowest rung of society as long as they don't have to be responsible for arduous tasks like getting an education and keeping a steady job. His pandering to the perceived weak and vulnerable further worsened their living conditions and bankrupted them of ambition. On the other hand, it solidified a voting bloc which was probably the goal to begin with. This legislation and its long term results are consistent with Democrats' primary objective of maintaining political power regardless of the cost. If used properly the program should be temporary assistance for people until they become self-sufficient and no longer need the assistance. My mother, Star Parker, and so many others should serve as examples that it can be done. However, the ease of assimilating to the welfare lifestyle and difficulty of adjusting to life without having many needs provided by someone else makes it easy to get comfortable. As we've discussed before, helping people rise above poverty is not in the best interest of the Democratic Party.

Who Benefits from the Black Community's Hardships?

Lyndon Johnson used a typical Democrat political strategy by politicizing people's hardships. Exploiting poverty is a great way to win votes from the less sophisticated. In recent years John Edwards has been the leading national Democrat that has adopted LBJ's strategy. He used the same strategy in his 2004 and 2008 presidential elections which resulted in him not getting his party's nomination. Unfortunately for him (and fortunately for the rest of us), this played out theme of declaring "war on poverty" alone just won't get you elected to the White House anymore.

• The Democrats have created political fortunes by exploiting the hardships of others primarily through the exploitation of poverty. When they mention poverty in speeches and in rhetoric there is a false assumption that poverty in America is comparable to global poverty. This is not the case. Growing up in West Palm Beach in what can be considered as American poverty and having lived in government provided housing and Section 8 vouchers, I believed that I was experiencing some of the worst conditions in the world. It wasn't until I joined the military and spent time in Egypt and Mexico that I realized just how much American's take for granted.

Liberals proved during the healthcare debate of 2009 that there is no depth they are not willing to stoop in order to advance their agenda of controlling the lives of everyone. It's common practice for them to exploit the uninformed, but they are also more than willing to exploit their own as well. Within hours of Senator Ted Kennedy's death on August 26, 2009, I got an email from MoveOn.org attempting to exploit their followers with more emotion baiting and demagoguery in hopes of using Kennedy's death as a rallying cry to force the American citizenry into accepting their takeover of our healthcare system and making him into a healthcare martyr. To those who think with their hearts, it would be a compelling message. To people like me who live in the real world, their message is a load of bull crap. The message said "Senator Teddy Kennedy passed away last night and our movement lost a hero... As we grieve, we must honor his memory and re-dedicate ourselves to his fight... Tonight, please light a candle in your window to memorialize him... Tomorrow, let's re-commit ourselves to achieving the thing that mattered most to him: Quality, affordable health care for every single American."[87] I suppose that the love of his wife and family was secondary to his quest for universal healthcare. Like with most things, you have to suspend disbelief in order for liberalism to make sense or have any credibility. As an

155

emancipated political slave, I can look at this for what it is. This is more mind control from thought leaders, using Saul Alinsky tactics to consolidate power by exploiting the fears and passion of the masses.

When my mother and I lived in Dunbar Village housing complex, we had running water, electricity, and food despite being considered poor. I got to see some of the living conditions in Egypt and I realized that having running water alone is a luxury that most Americans take for granted. When you add the fact that the water is clean it's even more impressive. As a cook in the military, we threw away a lot. At night we would set unwanted food and trash out to be picked up the next day by soldiers on details but most of the Egyptian desert people would come and take it away before they would get there. When we left our living areas, I noticed that a lot of the things we threw away were being used by the indigenous people. These experiences have had lasting effects on my perception of poverty and made me realize that the worst conditions in America are better than some of the best conditions in other places around the world. It also makes me angry to think that so many so-called "poor" Americans don't realize this.

In Mexico and in the Egyptian desert where I was stationed, I saw real poverty. A big part of American poverty is obesity. America has more than its share of fat poor people. I assume that there are other people in the world, especially those who are really poor, that will not be able to grasp this concept. Liberals will try to convince you that many of these people living in poverty can't "afford" to eat healthier. Nonetheless, the liberal mindset is to make excuses for everything and always find a villain to blame (particularly a conservative.) As House Financial Services Committee Chairman Rep. Barney Frank taught us when they can't find someone to blame, it can get frustrating, but they won't look in the mirror where the blame often belongs. In a hearing discussing the financial crisis and the government assisted takeover of a private company Merrill Lynch & Co. he admitted "Here is my problem. I cannot find a villain. Now, many of my colleagues have found various villains. They tend to be private sector or public sector, depending on the ideology of the finder. But, as I look at what happened, what I see is a very difficult situation that threatened further severe damage to an economy already damaged."[88] Democrats like him who are accustomed to throwing stones are flummoxed when their search for villains yields no results.

The liberal establishment wants you to believe that the 37 million people, approximately 12.6 percent of the total population,[89] that the government defines as "poor," live in conditions similar to the people that I encountered in the desert of Egypt or the streets of Mexico. The dirty little secret is that when liberals discuss poverty they are referring to Americans who live below the official poverty line, which is an annual income that they determine. That doesn't mean they are going without food, shelter and clothing, it means that they generate income at or below their designated amounts. In order to push their agenda, they exploit the "poor" for political gain by using sympathetic language like "millions more struggle to get by." They want you to equate American poverty to mothers and children living on the streets hungry, and unable to provide basic needs. The truth is that if American poverty means a lack of food, housing, and clothing, then very few of the 37 million people identified as living "in poverty" by the Census Bureau would be considered poor.

I had to be honest with myself when I compared how my mother and I lived, and how many of our other "poor" friends and family members lived. I realized that it wasn't so bad when compared to poverty abroad. In fact, things have gotten much better for "poor" people here in the United States. As technology improves and becomes more affordable and accessible, conditions of the "poor" have improved with the rest of society. Growing up in West Palm Beach I observed that many of my relatives, which liberals would categorize as "poor," chose not to work because it was more lucrative to exist using a combination of welfare checks, SSI, food stamps, housing assistance, free school lunch for the kids, odd jobs and "hustling" than they would a full-time job. The living conditions and quality-of-life can be much more appealing than trying to lure somebody into getting up early every day toiling for eight hours in hopes of an honest wage that can provide the equivalent to the taxpayer funded lifestyle that's been provided. Having visited the homes of many Section 8 recipients, I have noticed a common theme. Many of them have new furniture, the latest electronics, and contemporary fashion, while their children are failing in school, the parents don't have any work ethic and they spend their weekends having a good time. Of course this isn't everyone on Section 8, but I guarantee it's a great deal of them. When you are accustomed to not providing for your well being, you can easily fall into a pattern of buying what you want and begging others for what you need.

When liberals paint poverty in America with a broad brush they neglect to tell you that many of the so-called "people living in poverty" actually generate annual taxable salaries, which begs the question if they're truly poor. Yet, liberals continue to maintain the imagery that these individuals are living lives of misery and woe. Despite living in the category the liberals have given them, they are somehow able to find enough money to get into nightclubs which don't accept any government vouchers or offer financial assistance (excluding ladies' nights.) You can't show up to the club wearing rags so they have to find money for nice clothes and have money for drinks as well. When I go home to West Palm Beach, I always enjoy going to the 45th

Street Flea Market because it's always great to see just how wrong liberals are. The "Flea," as it is known, is always filled with people the liberals would consider "poor" getting their nails, hair and feet done, buying clothes from foreign vendors, purchasing the latest music and movies, getting glossy handbills for all of the latest parties and dining on local delicacies like (my favorites) mangoes with vinegar and conch salad. This is American poverty in action.

You have to examine the facts to realize how the United States taxpayer is being taken advantage of by the liberal establishment that pull at our heartstrings and make us feel guilty for not feeling sorrow for the millions of people who manipulate the system. They always try to convince taxpayers that they aren't doing enough. Without reform, entitlement spending for social programs risks bankrupting our treasury if left unchecked. You have to take away your biases and look at the facts when you examine poverty in America. If you do, you'll be disturbed at your findings, like I was. I believe that people that are really in need of assistance are the ones that work diligently on jobs where they make too much money to qualify for assistance and struggle to make ends meet. If the government provided any assistance it should be to help people caught in this type of wedge, as opposed to rewarding the behavior of people who have no desire to contribute anything meaningful to society. You'll find that many of the so-called "poor" live in better living conditions than the people that get up and work everyday. Their lack of desire and acceptance of low living standards keep them in a perpetual state of need where they will always qualify for any "low income" assistance. This is by liberal design and not coincidence.

The Heritage Foundation found that if you look closer, you'll find 46% of the 37 million people identified as living "in poverty" by the Census Bureau actually own their own homes.[90] The typical poor American has more living space than the average individual living in Paris, London, Vienna, Athens, and other cities throughout Europe. Nearly three-quarters of poor households own a car; 30 percent own two or more cars. Ninety-seven percent of poor households have a color television; over half own two or more color televisions. Seventy-eight percent have a VCR or DVD player; 62 percent have cable or satellite TV reception. Seventy-three percent own microwave ovens and a third have an automatic dishwasher.[91] Many of these people can't afford (or are unwilling to buy) school supplies so that their children are equipped with the tools needed to learn while somehow being able to afford to pay cell phone bills. Despite these material possessions, the liberals want you to believe that these people are living a horrible existence deprived of the basic necessities that Americans hold dear. Nonetheless, while the overwhelming majority of poor Americans don't live in conditions nearly as bad as the liberal establishment would like for us to believe, there are Americans who indeed are suffering in conditions comparable to the ones I experienced in Mexico and the desert ~~of each~~ of Egypt. We can't forget about these people who are truly suffering and we must work to help them as we can. Clearly, "poor" is culturally defined.

A Challenge to Liberal Leaders

I challenge the liberals to come with me to my hometown of West Palm Beach or any other city in this country and open up the doors to some of these people's houses who have their living expenses paid for by the taxpayer. You'll find many of these people living in conditions better than many working people. You'll also see that people will find the money to buy the latest gadgets, but no money to buy cleaning supplies. When I was young I was told that many "people buy what they want and beg for what they need." The older I get, the more I find that statement to be true primarily among people with a poverty mentality. I have relatives who seem to have embraced the cycle of poverty. Their entire lives are nearly (or fully) subsidized by the taxpayer which allows them to stay "fly" (in style) and enjoy the nightlife and "kick it" (relaxing) in the day waiting for something to happen. This allows them to lie around and have more babies for the taxpayers to pay for. With so much time on their hands, you would think their living areas would be immaculate, but that is not always the case. The liberals have snatched any incentive to live productive lives which even includes cleaning up your own living space. Many of these people, particularly young black men, wait for others to earn money and then rob them.

Growing up in West Palm Beach, every week it seemed as though I would hear another story about someone robbing Guatemalans, who are Hispanic laborers often targeted for robbery because they often carry large sums of cash after getting paid. They are also reluctant to report crimes and have a reputation for heavy drinking. Robbing happened so frequently it seemed like sport, but in recent years it has become deadly. Too often the perpetrators are young black men who seem to prey on the laborers. In one deadly incident *The Palm Beach Post* reported that Oliver Perez and three friends, already slightly drunk, decided to take a shortcut through "the cut," a footpath in the Hampton Court apartment complex, unaware that a group of stalkers were already in wait.[92] After a botched robbery the men ran from the four teenage robbers, and a gunshot was fired, killing Perez, 23 years old. Alfonso Gordon, 16, Kerry Willis, 15, and Stephon Davis, 19, are all charged with first-degree murder in the death of Oliver Levi Perez. Another man, 19-year-old Jermaine Donte Taylor, was also charged with another murder and admitted to being the shooter, according to a sheriff's report. Other recorded crimes against Guatemalans include robbers posing as immigration officers; a group of 11 young men, armed with a BB gun, that beat and robbed three Guatemalan landscapers; a 21-year-old Guatemalan man who was shot in the chest and killed in the north end of West Palm Beach after he struggled with two robbers, while his father was struck in the forehead with the gun; a 32-year-old Guatemalan man who was beaten to death in August by a group of teenagers in Fort Pierce as he called his family from a gas station's pay phone, and the list goes on.[93] Liberals have created this culture and benefit from these young black men that prey on others. They also make excuses for this behavior, which enables the behavior to continue, and further enables liberals to continue their exploitation.

The liberals designed the welfare system as a form of political slavery. Once you get in the cycle and develop the dependency lifestyle, as with anything else, it becomes hard to abandon. You don't realize it but you become a tool of the liberals and a key part of their propaganda machine. I read a tear jerking story about a Southside Chicago welfare recipient who stood outside a market at midnight, braving the spring chill for her first chance to buy groceries because her food stamps ran out. The story wants you to feel sorry for her because the weakening economy has put a strain on government dependents. The story describes her as a 23-year-old single mother, (which was her choice), who relies heavily on her $312 monthly allotment of food stamps - a ration adjusted just once a year, in

October. The $312 she gets from the government is more than the monthly food bill of my four person family. "Ain't got no food left, the kids are probably hungry," she said. Dennis Kladis opens "One Stop Food & Liquors" on the first of the month at midnight to cater to "desperate" families by giving them a chance to buy food as soon as possible. "I'm telling you, by the end of the month they're just dying to get back to the first," said Kladis, who has watched other area stores follow his lead.[94] "Obviously, they are struggling to get through the month." This is a clear demonstration of the unconscious dependency created by the liberal establishment. Keep in mind that $542 a month for a family of four is the maximum food stamp payment, yet people complain that it is not enough. This is much more than many working families can afford. This is more proof that you can't appease liberals when it comes to their socialist propaganda.

Perhaps the biggest tragedy of the liberal establishment's exploitation of poverty has been the creation of a mentality where people believe wholeheartedly that someone else should take care of them. For instance, it took a US Circuit Court of Appeals to decide that the victims of hurricane Katrina aren't legally entitled to a "continuing stream of payments." Three years after the hurricane, there are still people trying to milk checks from the government. After the judgment, some of the "survivors" threatened to file a claim against the federal government for $3 quadrillion.[95] People have endured natural

165

disasters for centuries. At some point you have to pick up the pieces and move on. The truth is that is many of these people were probably dependent on government before the storm. Their antics reaffirm their indoctrination, which teaches them that it is fully acceptable to live a life of excess at someone else's expense as long as you accept their authority over your life and you reward them with political undying loyalty. At times these elites will need to study you so that they can feel comfort knowing that they have done their best to bring equality to the world at your expense. This allows them to go back to their latte sipping, crack-free communities and have a guilt free slumber.

The Liberals have trained poor people to instinctively reject notions of their political enemies that try to instill the values of hard work, dignity and respect. They are not only instructed to reject self-improvement, they should lash out at the source no matter who the person is. This includes people of their own hue. In fact, it is counter productive to the liberal agenda when so-called impoverished people undo the work of the Democratic Party by starting to believe in personal responsibility and realize that hard work can be its own reward. If these government aided recipients begin to believe that they have power over poverty, the Democratic establishment will be ruined. They will find that the trade off of hard work and sacrifice in exchange for financial and personal freedom is more valuable the crumbs and security of getting just enough that the liberals offer. The good news for the impoverished, and the bad news for the Democratic Party, is that a lot of the poverty in the United States can be eliminated.

The Heritage Foundation found that the two primary culprits of poverty, particularly among children in the United States, are parents who don't work much and absent fathers. Regardless of the economic environment, the typical American "poor" family with children is supported by only 800 hours of work during a year which is the equivalent of 16 hours of work per week, which is much less than the standard 40 hour work week. If working hours in each family were raised to 2,000 hours per year, which is the equivalent of one adult working 40 hours per week throughout the year, approximately 75 percent of poor children would be lifted out of official poverty.[96] I can personally attest to the difficulties a single parent has trying to make ends meet. My mother struggled to take care of my sisters and I. Unfortunately our story is not unusual.

The absence of fathers in black households increases the likelihood of childhood poverty. Nearly two-thirds of poor children reside in single-parent homes; each year, an additional 1.3 million children are born out of wedlock.[97] The modern pop culture doesn't honor men who fulfill their duties as providers, but instead exalt men who are perceived as "fighters" and "lovers" (i.e. "thugs" and "gangsters.") This is why the thug and

Casanova images are so desirable among young men. Neither are naturally inclined to "settle down," so it is imperative that they don't stay still very long because they are not naturally inclined to be providers. Both stereotypes are only concerned with their own needs and live lives focused on achieving pleasure and self-gratification. Over time women have been forced to accept this type of behavior which has resulted in the acceptance of single-parenthood.

Esteemed motivational speaker and multi-millionaire Randy Gage defines the poverty mentality as subconscious programming that determines your approach to just about everything in life. Instead of being programmed for success, most people are programmed to avoid failure. Warning signs of the poverty mentality are the constant fixation on money, being jealous of all the things other people have, which ultimately turns into hate, and making decisions based on fear of loss or failure which never leads toward prosperity.[98] As a result of the poverty mentality programmed and reinforced by liberals, "poor" people will understandably never prosper in this country. Ironically, liberals cultivate class warfare among the "poor" and encourage them to direct their animosity towards so-called rich people, although many of these people still desire to be rich. If you don't believe me, listen to the urban music stations. Entertainers glamorize getting money, living in big homes like on MTV Cribs, and driving expensive cars. Kool G Rap expressed the plight of the work, risk and reward of capitalism magnificently in his 1980's classic rap song Road to Riches:

When I was five years old I realized there was a road
At the end I will win lots of pots of gold
Never took a break, never made a mistake
Took time to create 'cause there's money to make
To be a billionaire takes hard work for years
Some nights I shedded tears while I sent up prayers
Been through hard times, even worked part time
In a seafood store sweeping floors for dimes
I was sort of a porter taking the next man's order...
All my manpower for four bucks an hour
Took the time, I wrote rhymes in the shower
Shoes are scoffed (be)cause the road gets rough
But I'ma rock it til my pockets ain't stuffed enough
All the freaks wouldn't speak (be)cause my checks was weak
They would turn the other cheek so I started to seek
A way to get a play, and maybe one day
I'll be performing up a storm for a decent pay
No matter how it seems I always kept the dream...
Dreamed about it for five years straight
Finally I got a break and cut my first plate
The road ain't yellow and there ain't no witches
My name is Kool G Rap, I'm on the road to the riches [99]

The lifestyle the entertainer boasts cannot be acquired living on welfare. Our urban communities express their belief in capitalism and their desire for its fruit in their music yet liberals are out to convince them otherwise. This creates an inconsistent dynamic where becoming rich as an entertainer is good, while getting rich as a Fortune 500 CEO is bad. Liberals attempt to convince people that in a capitalist system, everyone can't have wealth, a case I won't argue. However, they try to also convince them that they CAN'T have it because of conditions beyond their control. That's where I disagree.

Although the poverty mentality may appear to be exclusive to the black community, it is not. It trickles throughout society and its impact has been devastating. The culture of poverty has now become glamorized and has affected how we speak and interact with one another. Black culture has been hijacked by "street" culture with its catchy jargon and style. Now with the rap music as its primary vehicle, "rappers" have taken the streets to Hollywood, the suburbs and now they've gone worldwide. There are now affluent children in Tokyo who probably believe that they are real gangsters like the "rapper" 50-Cent because they wear G-Unit clothes and know the lyrics to all of his songs. Now that rap has proven to be glamorous and lucrative it has resulted in legions of black men who believe that this manufactured image of a black man spawned from American poverty is their ticket to fortune and fame while so-called black leaders seem to collectively ignore this development.

Success is Reserved for the Few

You would think that promoting healthy families would be an important issue that Black Democrat leaders would embrace instead of relentlessly chasing the specter of racism. It doesn't even seem to be on the agenda. The collapse of the black family is one of the primary culprits for the miserable condition of many American cities. The truth is that many don't care about encouraging fathers to abandon negative images and take care of their responsibilities by marrying the mother of their children. Remember, keeping people in the cycle of poverty is a very lucrative profession. Al Sharpton and Jesse Jackson have been promoting the misery of black people in the board rooms of rich white people for years, while conditions for the people they are allegedly advocating for continuously to get worse under their "leadership." At the same time they have become millionaires, commanding big bucks for appearances, having corporate sponsorships, and full access to the American media. I don't know how much Mr. Sharpton is worth but he has to be "rich" because in 2008 the IRS hit him with a $931,397 federal tax bill and a $365,558 New York City tax bill according to an IRS lien.[100] That's more than many people make in a lifetime. He needs to hurry up and pay his taxes because the $1.3 million he owes will help a lot of the needy people he advocates for to get free health care, food stamps, fair housing and fair union pay.

Unfortunately for America, Barack Obama is picking up where these two left off in regards to fixing poverty. At first, (I'll begrudgingly admit) I was beginning to believe the hype about Barack Obama, thinking that he would be the one who could transcend partisan politics by offering a new vision for this country. He quickly proved me wrong by showing himself to be a typical brainwashed liberal, especially when it comes to issues of poverty. He offers more expensive versions of policies that have increased Democrats voting majorites but have failed in the past. He is nothing new. He is just a carefully manufactured product of Democrat strategist, telepromters and the help of the media. When you read his website as I did, you will find that his answers to fixing poverty is forcing the taxpayer to fund his attempts at being benevolent. His entire plan will add billions on top of the already billions of dollars that this government pays to combat poverty. Like the rest of the liberals, he cites the number of 37 million poor people which are the people we've mentioned in earlier chapters. He wants you to think that they are living in the same conditions as the people I encountered while in Egypt, when we all know this is not true. He and his wife want you to think that there are no opportunities in America, and only select black people like them have have the internal fortitude to succeed. The rest of us unfortunate Negroes are doomed to failure without liberal intervention because we weren't blessed with the fortitude shared by people like the Obamas, Henry Gates, Michael Dyson and Mark Hill. This is textbook political exploitation of the poor, perfected by the Democratic Party. His campaign became comical because he (by design) became the fill-in-the blank candidate. Change was deceptively ambiguous because it allowed so many people to personally define it, and Obama became the personification of it.

They don't want you to know the reality of American poverty. The truth is that millions of people are exploited so that the larger voting population can feel sympathy for people who have no desire to ever work or get off public assistance. Obama wants you to believe that if the federal government, led by him of course, spends millions more on what he calls "Access to Jobs." Then people living in poverty will all of a sudden have the will and desire to make something of their lives because of the election of a messianic Barack Obama, whose own mother was on welfare (which the liberals like to remind us.) After the high of the Obama campaign started to wear off and the reality of rising unemployment set in, hopeful people like Jeff Fravor, a retired train conductor from Ohio, who put their faith in this man found out what I already knew. "People were looking for a savior to get us out of this mess and that's why they voted for Obama. I've [got] nothing against Obama personally, but he's new to the job and 'hope' won't fix this mess," he said.[101] Anyone with any sense knows that Obama's undefined notion of hope and change are foolish and wishful thinking at best. There is not enough money in the world to make someone do anything that they don't want to do. There are already countless jobs and opportunities that many of these 37 million people refuse to take advantage of because of the culture of failure that many have been born into, and that they have embraced. Ignorance is bliss and, believe me, there is a lot of bliss amongst the impoverished in this country.

I have many relatives who have never worked or ever had the desire to become productive citizens. Many are career criminals and habitual substance abusers, yet they always have somewhere to stay, have food, and money in their pocket. All or some of these are subsidized by the government in some way. Many people know about Section 8 housing and food stamps, but many don't know about SSI. The United States Social Security administration provides what is called Supplemental Security Income (SSI) which are payments to people with low income who are age 65 or older or have a disability.[102] When you hear disabilities you may assume they mean severe disabilities, such as rare diseases and physical ailments which make functioning in a normal capacity nearly impossible. In addition to severe disabilities they also force taxpayers to pay for someone's desire to abuse illegal drugs, children who are born with minor speech impediments, illegal aliens and many other creative things people think of in order to avoid having to work an honest job. The definition of disability is purposely broad which can be interpreted as an invitation to fraud and leads to hard-earned taxpayer dollars being wasted.

In 2008, The Oregonian found in an ongoing investigation of the Social Security Administration that it has fallen behind in reviewing the medical conditions of 1.7 million Americans on its disability rolls which could result in potentially paying up to $11 billion in benefits to people who are no longer disabled. Historically, the reviews have a phenomenal rate of return. In 2007 it saved $11.74 for every $1 spent, according to agency records. The promise of open-ended payments, objective standards and limited oversight invites fraud. Some of the more dramatic cases include Denise M. "Dee" Henderson, a Minnesota mom who received SSI after a car accident and claimed she couldn't stand for more than ten minutes. A month later, she won the Mrs. Minnesota International pageant after taking part in an evening gown competition and an aerobic wear fashion show. In 2004, a jury found Henderson guilty of nine counts of defrauding Social Security and a judge sent her to prison. Other cases include an Oregon woman who got regular disability benefits for a bad back and later competed as an equestrian; a pair of New Jersey business partners who claimed mental and physical conditions and later launched a restaurant specializing in gourmet soups; and a Florida woman who was awarded disability benefits because of her legal blindness and later renewed her driver's license and was busted for fraud after getting two traffic tickets.[103]

The government is aware that fraud is inevitable so they try to prevent it. The government puts out pamphlets with a lot of legal mumbo-jumbo stating all of the severe penalties for falsifying documents. These people could care less about these threats and call the government's bluff every time. It's almost like the government encourages giving away taxpayer money via cash assistance because they make the eligibility so easy to meet. They also offer links and access to get more free stuff from the government. They are also eligible for automatic cost-of-living adjustments, something that many wage earners don't even get. This naturally discourages productivity, yet the liberals in this country want to increase the budgets for this type of behavior because it only solidifies their voting base by subduing the human spirit's innate desire to live a fulfilling life.

Let me reiterate that I understand that there is a place for government assistance and some people are truly in need. However, I have seen firsthand abuse of the system by people that are capable of contributing to society but choose not to. This is enabled by liberals and encouraged simply because success begets success. It would be catastrophic for their electoral strategy if the people they manipulate (although they say "advocate") start to realize their personal power and exchange their freedom for their golden handcuffs.

7

NOTES

<u>**Chapter 1: The Purpose of This Book**</u>

---

[1] Geraghty, Jim, "Edwards: 'Pretty Soon We're Not Going to Have a Young African-American Male Population in America.'" Nationalreview.com September 28, 2007
http://campaignspot.nationalreview.com/post/?q=Yjk3OGY3MDl4NjcyMGZjZjhjZTY2NDhmZTlkODhkMWI=

Youtube: http://www.youtube.com/watch?v=OtC96Jzy90g

[2] Hulsey, Lynn. "Democratic party leader implores students to go vote, immediately" Dayton Daily News October 22, 2008
http://www.daytondailynews.com/n/content/oh/story/news/local/2008/10/22/ddn102208dean.html

[3] Quaint, Michael. "New York's Paterson, Lawmakers Agree on State Budget (Update3)" Bloomberg.com Apr 9, 2008
http://www.bloomberg.com/apps/news?pid=20601103&sid=aJn6GX6TqpkU&refer=us#

[4] Primary Source, "Obama Signs Lilly Ledbetter Act" WashingtonPost.com January 29, 2009
http://voices.washingtonpost.com/44/2009/01/29/obama_signs_lilly_ledbetter_ac.html

[5] "Obama signs 'Lilly Ledbetter Fair Pay Act'" USAToday.com January 29, 2009
http://content.usatoday.com/communities/theoval/post/2009/01/62099146/1

[6] Seib, Gerald F. "In Crisis, Opportunity for Obama" Wall Street Journal November 21, 2008
http://online.wsj.com/article/SB122721278056345271.html?mod=googlenews_wsj#

[7] Weisman, Jonathan. "Emanuel Sets a Challenge" November 19, 2008 Wall Street Journal
http://online.wsj.com/article/SB122706319966040053.html

[8] The Hermitage- Home of President Andrew Jackson- Slavery
http://www.thehermitage.com/index.php?option=com_content&task=view&id=36&Itemid=49

<u>**Chapter 2: Who is Andre Harper?**</u>

[9] Brody, David. "Obama Says He Doesn't Want His Daughters Punished with a Baby" March 31, 2008 Christian Broadcasting Network
http://www.cbn.com/cbnnews/348569.aspx

Youtube Clip: http://www.youtube.com/watch?v=GbZJYWjkAPo

[10] The Church of the Living God, the Pillar and Ground of the Truth, Inc. :Church History:
http://clgpgt.org/ORG/hist1.html

[11] "Charleston Black Heritage" The Official Visitors' Guide for African-American Tourism in Charleston, South Carolina- History Page- Gullah
http://www.charlestonblackheritage.com/gullah.html

[12] Barton, Antigone and Gilken, Rochelle E.B. "Seventh-grader arrested in gang rape; police seek nine more teens" Palm Beach Post Wednesday, July 04, 2007
http://www.palmbeachpost.com/news/content/local_news/epaper/2007/07/04/s1a_RAPE_ARREST_0704.html

Chapter 3: Escaping the Plantation

[13] Sasse, Benjamin and Weems, Kerry. "The Return of Welfare As We Knew It" The Wall Street Journal February 10, 2009
http://online.wsj.com/article/SB123422835499665849.html

[14] Sommer, Joseph C. "Ohio Democratic Party is no longer the 'party of the people'" The Plain Dealer August 08, 2009
http://blog.cleveland.com/letters/2009/08/ohio_democratic_party_is_no_lo.html

[15] Bowman, John. "The History of The American Presidency." North Dayton, MA: World Publications Group, Inc. 1998.

[16] Garvey, Marcus. "Message To The People: The Course of African Philosophy" Dover MA: the Majority Press, 1986

[17] Lewis, Monica. "Unions with Highest Number of Black Workers Face Major Questions" BlackAmericaWeb.com July 26, 2005
http://www.blackamericaweb.com/site.aspx/bawnews/unions727

[18] ibid

[19] Garvey, Marcus. "Message To The People: The Course of African Philosophy" Dover MA: the Majority Press, 1986

[20] Kirsanow, Peter "The Florida Myth." NationalReview.com October 15, 2003
http://www.nationalreview.com/comment/kirsanow200310150822.asp

[21] Timmerman, Kenneth R. Shakedown: Exposing The Real Jesse Jackson. Washington, DC: Regnery Publishing, Inc. 2002.

[22] McLaughlin, Eliott C. "Harare woman: 'If you talk too much... they hunt you down'" CNN http://www.cnn.com/2008/WORLD/africa/06/25/zimbabwe.voices/index.html

[23] "Ohio Secretary Of State Office Rebukes Obama Campaign" 4 Mar 2008
http://marcambinder.theatlantic.com/archives/2008/03/ohio_secretary_of_state_rebukes_obama_campaign.php

[24] ibid.

[25] Wills, Christopher. "Trinity UCC Gets Increased Security" Black America Web April 03, 2008
http://www.blackamericaweb.com/site.aspx/headlines/trinitythreats404

[26] Malcolm X House Negro
Youtube Clip: http://www.youtube.com/watch?v=znQe9nUKzvQ

[27] The Urban Dictionary: House Nigger
http://www.urbandictionary.com/define.php?term=house%20nigger

[28] Poor, Jeff. "House Majority Whip: Climate Change Hurts Blacks More"
Business & Media Institute 29 July 2008
http://www.businessandmedia.org/printer/2008/20080729130950.aspx

[29] Associated Press. "Obama Backs Away From McCain Town Hall Challenge" Fox News August 2, 2008
http://elections.foxnews.com/2008/08/02/obama-campaign-accepts-3-debates-with-mccain/

[30] "Biden predicts early crisis will test Obama" CNN.com, October 20, 2008
http://politicalticker.blogs.cnn.com/2008/10/20/biden-predicts-early-crisis-will-test-obama/

[31] Snow, Mary and Crowley, Candy. "Clinton's 'Plantation' Remark Draws Fire."
CNN.com, 18 January 2006,
http://www.cnn.com/2006/POLITICS/01/17/clinton.plantation/

[32] Ibid

[33] National Action Network: About
http://www.nationalactionnetwork.net/about.html

[34] The National Association for the Advancement of Colored People- Our Mission
http://www.naacp.org/about/mission/index.htm

Chapter 4: I am a Republican Because...

[35] X, Malcolm. "God's Judgment of White America (The Chickens Come Home to Roost)" MalcolmX.org December 4 , 1963 http://www.malcolm-x.org/speeches/spc_120463.htm

[36] http://www.democrats.org/a/party/history.html (as of January 2008)

[37] TMZ Staff. "Perez vs. Will.I.Am -- CAUGHT ON TAPE" TMZ.com June 22, 2009
http://www.tmz.com/2009/06/22/perez-vs-will-i-am-caught-on-tape/

[38] Tapper, Jake. "McCain to Attack Obama for Public Radio Comments From 2001"
ABC News.com October 27, 2008
http://blogs.abcnews.com/politicalpunch/2008/10/mccain-to-attac.html

[39] Email from President Obama- sent Wed 8/05/09 1:46 PM

Paid for by Organizing for America, a project of the Democratic National Committee --
430 South Capitol Street SE, Washington, D.C. 20003.

[40] AP. "White House Vows to Defend Democrats on Health Reform, Will 'Punch Back
Twice as Hard'" Fox News August 07, 2009
http://www.foxnews.com/politics/2009/08/07/health-punch-back/

[41] Phillips, Macon. "Facts Are Stubborn Things" Whitehouse.gov August 4, 2009
http://www.whitehouse.gov/blog/Facts-Are-Stubborn-Things/

[42] Stephey, M.J. & Pickert, Kate. "Rahm Emanuel" Time.com November 6, 2008
http://www.time.com/time/politics/article/0,8599,1856965,00.html

[43] http://www.democrats.org/a/party/history.html (as of January 2008)

[44] Gross, Samantha and Barrett, Delvin. "Spitzer Got Tripped Up Laws He Enforced"
Breitbart.com March 11, 2008
http://www.breitbart.com/article.php?id=D8VBF6OO0&show_article=1

[45] Gattuso, James L. "Back to Muzak? Congress and the Un-Fairness Doctrine" The
Heritage Foundation May 23, 2007

[46] Ibid.

[47] "Her Royal Fairness" The American Spectator May 14, 2007
http://spectator.org/archives/2007/05/14/her-royal-fairness

[48] "Rush Announces eBay Charity Auction of Harry Reid's Letter" Rushlimbaugh.com
October 12, 2007
http://www.rushlimbaugh.com/home/daily/site_101207/content/01125114.guest.html

[49] "Dean defends imitation of Rush" The Washington Times May 22, 2005
http://www.washingtontimes.com/news/2005/may/22/20050522-115723-9021r/

[50] Hurt, Charles. "PREZ ZINGS GOP FOE IN A $TIMULATING TALK" New York
Post
January 23, 2009
http://www.nypost.com/seven/01232009/news/politics/prez_zings_gop_foe_in_a_timulat
ing_talk_151572.htm

[51] Democratic Congressional Campaign Committee
http://www.dccc.org/page/petition/rush

[52] http://womenshistory.about.com/cs/quotes/a/qu_h_clinton.htm

[53] Mooney, Alexander. "Dems launch anti-Limbaugh petition" CNN.com January 28,
2009
http://politicalticker.blogs.cnn.com/2009/01/28/dems-launch-anti-limbaugh-
petition/#comments

[54] McCormick, John and Zuckman, Jill. "Obama warns of overconfidence" Chicago Tribune
October 17, 2008
www.chicagotribune.com/news/nationworld/chi-campaign_daily17oct17,0,1997556,story

Obama Mocks Joe the Plumber, Crowd Laughs
http://www.youtube.com/watch?v=Sqis9mRcW14

[55] Ibanga, Imaeyen and Goldman, Russell. "America's Overnight Sensation Joe the Plumber Owes $1,200 in Taxes" ABCNews.com Oct. 16, 2008
http://abcnews.go.com/GMA/Vote2008/story?id=6047360&page=1

[56] Hershey, William. "Four more workers disciplined in "Joe the Plumber" snooping case" Dayton Daily News November 21, 2008
http://www.daytondailynews.com/o/content/shared-gen/blogs/dayton/ohiopolitics/entries/2008/11/21/four_more_workers_disciplined.html

[57] "Republicans Protest Congressional Vacation as Gas Prices Soar" ABC News
August 05, 2008
http://blogs.abcnews.com/politicalradar/2008/08/republicans-pro.html

Chapter 5: Re-Writing Black History

[58] Wormser, Richard. "Democratic Party" The Rise and Fall of Jim Crow Series- PBS.org
http://www.pbs.org/wnet/jimcrow/stories_org_democratic.html

[59] Darlene Clark Hine, William C. Hine, Stanley Harrold. "The African-American Odyssey: combined volume second edition" Prentice-Hall, upper saddle River, New Jersey 2003, Pearson education Inc.

[60] Democrat Leadership: http://www.democrats.org/a/party/ourleaders.html (as of August 7, 2008)

[61] http://www.democrats.org/a/party/history.html

[62] Wormser, Richard. "Democratic Party" The Rise and Fall of Jim Crow Series- PBS.org
http://www.pbs.org/wnet/jimcrow/stories_org_democratic.html

[63] Ibid.

[64] Wormser, Richard. "Republican Party" The Rise and Fall of Jim Crow Series- PBS.org
http://www.pbs.org/wnet/jimcrow/stories_org_republican.html

[65] Ibid.

[66] Ibid.

[67] Wormser, Richard. "Ku Klux Klan" The Rise and Fall of Jim Crow Series- PBS.org
http://www.pbs.org/wnet/jimcrow/stories_org_kkk.html

[68] Ibid.

[69] Wormser, Richard. "Democratic Party" The Rise and Fall of Jim Crow Series- PBS.org
http://www.pbs.org/wnet/jimcrow/stories_org_democratic.html

[70] Christensen, Jen. "FBI Tracked King's Every Move"
CNN.com March 31, 2008
http://www.cnn.com/2008/US/03/31/mlk.fbi.conspiracy/index.html#cnnSTCVideo

[71] Ibid.

[72] The Voting Rights Act of 1965- United States Department of Justice
http://www.usdoj.gov/crt/voting/intro/intro_b.php

[73] Clymer, Adam. "Herman Talmadge, Georgia Senator and Governor, Dies at 88" New York Times March 22, 2002
http://query.nytimes.com/gst/fullpage.html?res=9C04E3D81E38F931A15750C0A9649C8B63&sec=&spon=&pagewanted=2

[74] Alabama Governor, Inaugural addresses and programs, SP194, Alabama Department of Archives and History
http://www.archives.state.al.us/govs_list/InauguralSpeech.html

[75] The University of Mississippi- Department of Education
http://www.olemiss.edu/depts/south/ms_encyclopedia/sovereigntysample.htm

[76] Ibid.

Chapter 6: Don't Let the Liberals Fool You: American Poverty Isn't the Same

[77] Goldblatt, Jeff. "Obama's Former Pastor Getting $1.6M Home in Retirement"
FOXNews.com March 27, 2008
http://elections.foxnews.com/2008/03/27/obamas-former-pastor-builds-a-multimillion-dollar-retirement-home/

[78] "'Joe the plumber' getting smeared, McCain says" CNN.com October 17, 2008
http://politicalticker.blogs.cnn.com/2008/10/17/joe-the-plumber-getting-smeared-mccain-says/#comments

[79] Henneberg, Molly. "D.C. Families Bemoan Imminent Loss of Voucher Program"
FOXNews.com April 14, 2009
http://www.foxnews.com/politics/2009/04/14/dc-families-bemoan-imminent-loss-voucher-program/

[80] Ibid.

[81] "D.C. Council Wants Vouchers" The Wall Street Journal July 14, 2009
http://online.wsj.com/article/SB124743971109829635.html

[82] Turque, Bill and Murray, Shailagh. "Obama Offers D.C. Voucher Compromise"
The Washington Post May 7, 2009

http://www.washingtonpost.com/wp-
dyn/content/article/2009/05/06/AR2009050603852.html

[83] Bovard James, *Freedom in Chains: The Rise of the State and the Demise of the Citizen* (New York: St. Martin's 2000), pg. 68 citing US Department of Agriculture, *Food and Nutrition*, Feb 1972

[84] Ibid.

[85] Pine, Lester and Pine, Tina. "Claudine" 20th Century Fox 1974 Directed by John Berry

[86] Bennish, Steve. "Technology helps gangs go hi-tech" Dayton Daily News February 18, 2008
http://www.daytondailynews.com/green/content/oh/story/news/local/2008/02/17/ddn0218
08daytongangsoldiers.html

[87] Email from Justin Ruben. "Teddy Kennedy" MoveOn.org Political Action Sent on August 26, 2009 2:24 PM http://pol.moveon.org/

[88] "Barney Frank Can't Find a Villain!" RushLimbaugh.com July 21, 2009
http://www.rushlimbaugh.com/home/daily/site_072109/content/01125107.guest.html

[89] "The Poverty Epidemic in America, by the Numbers" Americanprogress.org April 24, 2007
http://www.americanprogress.org/issues/2007/04/poverty_numbers.html

[90] Rector, Robert. "How Poor Are America's Poor? Examining the "Plague" of Poverty in America" The Heritage Foundation August 27, 2007
http://www.heritage.org/Research/Welfare/bg2064.cfm

[91] Ibid.

[92] Marra, Andrew. "3 more charged in April murder of Guatemalan man in Mangonia Park" The Palm Beach Post May 21, 2009
http://www.palmbeachpost.com/search/content/local_news/epaper/2009/05/21/0521guate
malanattack.html

[93] Heimericks, Niels. "Guatemalans often targeted for robberies" The Palm Beach Post May 21, 2009
http://www.palmbeachpost.com/localnews/content/local_news/epaper/2009/05/21/9521g
uatemalanattacks.html

[94] Babwin, Don. "Food stamp recipients pinched by high food prices" The Seattle Times May 19, 2008
http://seattletimes.nwsource.com/html/nationworld/2004423780_webfoodstamps19.html

[95] Kunzelman, Michael. "Katrina's Victims Ask for Huge Checks" Newsvine.com January 9, 2008
http://www.newsvine.com/_news/2008/01/09/1214007-katrinas-victims-ask-for-huge-
checks

[96] Rector, Robert. "How Poor Are America's Poor? Examining the "Plague" of Poverty in America" The Heritage Foundation August 27, 2007
http://www.heritage.org/Research/Welfare/bg2064.cfm

[97] Ibid.

[98] Gage, Randy. "Three Warning Signs of Poverty Mentality" Getmotivation.com
http://www.getmotivation.com/prosperity/randygage-poverty-mentality.html

[99] Kool G Rap. "Road To The Riches lyrics" lyricstime.com
http://www.lyricstime.com/kool-g-rap-road-to-the-riches-lyrics.html

[100] Bennett, Chuck. "SUBPOENA BLITZ PUTS HEAT ON AL" The New York Post
June 19, 2008
http://www.nypost.com/php/pfriendly/print.php?url=http://www.nypost.com/seven/06192
008/news/regionalnews/subpoena_blitz_puts_heat_on_al_116165.htm

[101] Carey, Nick. "As U.S. recession bites, Ohio hopes fade for Obama" Reuters.com
July 30, 2009
http://www.reuters.com/article/topNews/idUSTRE56T0SU20090730

[102] SSI- BASIC ELIGIBILITY FOR BENEFITS, Sec. 1602. [42 U.S.C. 1381a] Social Security Administration
http://www.ssa.gov/OP_Home/ssact/title16b/1602.htm

[103] Denson, Bryan and Walth, Brent. "Cheaters cost Social Security billions" The Oregonian
December 6, 2008
http://www.oregonlive.com/news/index.ssf/2008/12/disability_fraud_saps_social_s.html

Breinigsville, PA USA
01 December 2010
250429BV00004B/156/P